D1639428

Cook's Corner

Quick
& Easy

igloobooks

igloobooks

Published in 2018
by Igloo Books Ltd
Cottage Farm
Sywell
NN6 0BJ
www.igloobooks.com

Food photography and recipe development:
© Stockfood, The Food Media Agency
Cover image: © iStock / Getty Images
Additional imagery: © iStock / Getty Images

STA002 0618
2 4 6 8 10 9 7 5 3
ISBN: 978-1-78810-182-0

Cover designed by Nicholas Gage
Interiors designed by Simon Parker
Edited by Jasmin Peppiatt

Printed and manufactured in China

Cook's Corner

Quick & Easy

Contents

Cook's Corner

Quick & Easy

Breakfasts

Speedy eggs Benedict

SERVES: 4 | PREP TIME: 10 MINUTES | COOKING TIME: 8 MINUTES

INGREDIENTS

2 English breakfast muffins, halved

4 large eggs

2 tbsp butter, softened

4 slices smoked back bacon

8 green or white asparagus spears

FOR THE HOLLANDAISE SAUCE:

2 large egg yolks

2 tbsp lemon juice

125 g / 4 ½ oz / ½ cup butter

METHOD

1. Toast the muffin halves and keep warm in a low oven. Fry the bacon and asparagus in a large frying pan for 6 minutes, turning regularly.

2. Meanwhile, bring a wide saucepan of water to a gentle simmer. Crack each egg into a cup and pour it smoothly into the water, one by one. Simmer gently for 3 minutes then remove from the pan with a slotted spoon.

3. Butter the muffin halves and top with the bacon and asparagus. Sit a poached egg on top of each one and keep warm in a low oven while you make the hollandaise.

4. Put the yolks in a small measuring jug, just slightly larger in diameter than your immersion blender. Stir in the lemon juice and season with salt and white pepper.

5. Heat the butter in a small saucepan until it melts and starts to sizzle. Put the immersion blender into the egg yolk jug and turn it on, then pour in the hot butter in a thin stream.

6. As soon as all of the butter is incorporated, spoon it over the poached eggs and serve.

Cheese and broccoli omelette

SERVES: 1 | PREP TIME: 5 MINUTES | COOKING TIME: 10 MINUTES

INGREDIENTS

½ head of broccoli, florets only

4 eggs

salt and ground black pepper

2 tbsp butter

50 g / 1 ¾ oz / ½ cup Cheddar cheese, grated

METHOD

1. Place the broccoli florets into a pan of salted boiling water and cook for 6–8 minutes until tender. Drain and set aside until needed.

2. Whisk the eggs and season with salt and black pepper.

3. Melt the butter in a non-stick frying pan over a medium heat. Once foaming add the eggs and move around the pan so that they completely cover it.

4. Cook for 5 minutes until the top of the omelette is no longer runny, give the pan a gentle shake to ensure that the omelette has not stuck. Sprinkle over the grated cheese and add the broccoli to the omelette before seasoning to taste.

5. Carefully slide the omelette onto a serving plate, folding it in half as you transfer it.

Porridge with caramelized banana

SERVES: 1 | PREP TIME: 5 MINUTES | COOKING TIME: 10 MINUTES

INGREDIENTS

75 g / 2 ½ oz / ¾ cup whole porridge oats

200 ml / 7 fl. oz / ¾ cup almond milk

50 ml / 1 ¾ fl. oz / ¼ cup double (heavy) cream

1 tbsp honey

1 tbsp butter

1 tbsp honey

1 banana, sliced

1 tsp cinnamon

25 g almonds, chopped

METHOD

1. Place the oats and almond milk into a saucepan. Place onto the heat and bring up to boiling point whilst stirring, once thickened turn the heat down and mix through the cream and honey.

2. Heat the butter in a non-stick frying pan over a medium heat. Once foaming add the honey and stir through the butter.

3. Sprinkle the bananas with the cinnamon and add to the butter and honey mixture. Fry for 1–2 minutes until starting to colour before flipping over and cooking for a further minute.

4. Spoon the porridge into bowls and top with the bananas and chopped almonds.

13

Greek yogurt with honey and berries

SERVES: 2 | PREP TIME: 5 MINUTES

INGREDIENTS

500 ml / 17 ½ fl. oz / 2 cups natural yogurt

1 kiwi fruit, peeled, halved and sliced

6 strawberries, sliced

1 large handful blueberries

50 ml / 1 ¾ fl. oz / ¼ cup manuka honey

METHOD

1. Divide the yogurt between two bowls and stir in half the fruit.

2. Top with the rest of the fruit and drizzle with manuka honey.

Peach, thyme and goat's cheese crostini

MAKES: 6 | PREP TIME: 5 MINUTES | COOKING TIME: 4 MINUTES

INGREDIENTS

6 thin slices baguette

100 g / 3 ½ oz / 1 cup crumbly goat's cheese

1 ripe peach, quartered, stoned and sliced

a few sprigs fresh thyme

METHOD

1. Toast the baguette slices under a hot grill until golden brown.

2. Top with the goat's cheese and peach slices.

3. Strip the thyme leaves from the stems and sprinkle them over the top. Serve immediately.

Prosciutto, gruyère and thyme toasts

SERVES: 2 | PREP TIME: 5 MINUTES | COOKING TIME: 5 MINUTES

INGREDIENTS

4 slices sourdough bread

4 slices prosciutto

100 g / 3 ½ oz / 1 cup Gruyère cheese, grated

1 tbsp fresh thyme leaves

METHOD

1. Preheat the grill to its highest setting.

2. Toast the sourdough on one side under the grill.

3. Turn them over and top each one with a slice of prosciutto, the cheese and a sprinkle of thyme.

4. Grill for 2 more minutes or until the cheese is bubbling and the bread is toasted at the edges.

Bacon, egg and cheese baps

SERVES: 4 | PREP TIME: 5 MINUTES | COOKING TIME: 5 MINUTES

INGREDIENTS

8 rashers streaky bacon

1 tbsp butter

3 large eggs, beaten

4 slices processed cheese

4 white baps, halved horizontally

2 tbsp tomato ketchup

METHOD

1. Cook the bacon under a hot grill until crisp on both sides.

2. Meanwhile, heat the butter in a non-stick frying pan. When it starts to sizzle, pour in the beaten eggs.

3. When the egg starts to set at the bottom of the pan, draw the sides in with a spatula and tilt the pan to fill the furrows with more liquid egg.

4. When the egg is almost set on top, turn the omelette over with a spatula and cook the other side for 30 seconds.

5. Top the bap bottoms with processed cheese. Cut the omelette into quarters and divide between the baps, then arrange the bacon on top.

6. Spread the inside of the bap lids with ketchup and arrange on top. Serve immediately.

Muesli biscuits

MAKES: 6 | PREP TIME: 10 MINUTES | COOKING TIME: 20 MINUTES

INGREDIENTS

100 g / 3 ½ oz / ¼ cup butter
100 g / 3 ½ oz / ½ cup light brown sugar
300 g / 10 ½ oz / 2 ½ cups fruit and nut muesli

METHOD

1. Preheat the oven to 170°C (150° fan) /340F / gas 3.

2. Put the butter and sugar in a small saucepan and heat together until melted, stirring to dissolve the sugar. Stir in the muesli.

3. When the mixture is cool enough to handle, press it into 6 patties with your hands and space them out on a baking tray.

4. Bake for 20 minutes or until the biscuits are firm and lightly golden on top.

Pancakes

SERVES: 2 | PREP TIME: 10 MINUTES | COOKING TIME: 10 MINUTES

INGREDIENTS

150 g / 5 ¼ oz / 1 cup plain (all-purpose) flour

2 tbsp sugar

1 egg, beaten

200 ml / 7 fl. oz / ¾ cup milk

1 tbsp oil, for frying

chocolate sauce, honey and fruit, to serve

METHOD

1. Preheat the oven to its lowest setting.

2. In a large mixing bowl combine the flour and sugar.

3. Mix the egg and milk and pour into the dry ingredients. Whisk for a couple of minutes until a thick and smooth batter forms. Leave to stand for a couple of minutes.

4. Heat the oil in a non-stick frying pan over a medium high heat. Once hot, ladle the batter into the pan. Allow to form a pancake shape and cook for 1-2 minutes until small holes appear on the surface. Flip over and cook for a further minute before transferring to the oven to keep warm while you cook the remaining batter.

5. Serve the pancakes with a topping of your choice such as chocolate sauce, honey or fresh fruit.

French toast bites

SERVES: 2 | PREP TIME: 5 MINUTES | COOKING TIME: 10 MINUTES

INGREDIENTS

2 eggs, lightly beaten

50 ml / 1 ¾ fl. oz / ¼ cup double (heavy) cream

½ tsp cinnamon

½ tsp nutmeg

1 tsp vanilla extract

4 slices of bread

200 g / 7 oz. natural yogurt

2 tbsp raspberry jam (jelly)

50 g / 1 ¾ oz. / ⅓ cup fresh raspberries

METHOD

1. Combine the egg, cream, cinnamon, nutmeg and vanilla in a large bowl.

2. Soak the bread in the egg mixture taking care not to let it get too soggy.

3. Heat a frying pan over a medium heat, fry the bread for a couple of minutes on each side or until caramelised.

4. Remove from the pan and chop into bite sized pieces.

5. Place onto serving plates with the yogurt, jam and fresh raspberries.

Blueberry yogurt pots

SERVES: 5 | PREPARATION TIME: 5 MINUTES

INGREDIENTS

400 g / 14 oz / 1 ⅔ cups blueberry yogurt

100 g / 3 ½ oz / 1 cup granola

4 tbsp condensed milk

50 g / 1 ¾ oz / ⅓ cup blueberries

METHOD

1. Divide half the yogurt between four glasses and top with the granola.

2. Top with the rest of the yogurt, then add a tablespoon of condensed milk to each one and sprinkle over the blueberries.

Summer fruit crêpes

SERVES: 4 | PREP TIME: 5 MINUTES | COOKING TIME: 20 MINUTES

INGREDIENTS

150 g / 5 ½ oz / 1 cup plain (all-purpose) flour

1 large egg

325 ml / 11 ½ fl. oz / 1 ½ cups whole milk

30 g butter, melted

FOR THE FILLING:

3 tbsp redcurrant jelly (jello)

200 g / 7 oz / 1 cup mixed summer berries

METHOD

1. To make the filling, melt the redcurrant jelly in a small saucepan and stir in the fruit. Leave to macerate.

2. Sieve the flour into a bowl and make a well in the centre. Break in the egg and pour in the milk then use a whisk to gradually incorporate all of the flour from around the outside.

3. Melt the butter in a small frying pan then whisk it into the batter.

4. Put the buttered frying pan back over a low heat. Add a small ladle of batter and swirl the pan to coat the bottom.

5. When it starts to dry and curl up at the edges, turn the pancake over with a spatula and cook the other side until golden brown and cooked through.

6. Repeat with the rest of the mixture then serve each crêpe rolled up with a big spoonful of summer fruits inside.

Sausage patty and egg muffins

SERVES: 4 | PREP TIME: 15 MINUTES | COOKING TIME: 12 MINUTES

INGREDIENTS

250 g / 9 oz / 1 ⅔ cups minced turkey

250 g / 9 oz / 1 ⅔ cups pork sausagemeat

50 g / 1 ¼ oz / ⅔ cup fresh white breadcrumbs

1 tsp fresh sage leaves, finely chopped

1 egg yolk

To serve:

2 tbsp sunflower oil

4 large eggs

4 English breakfast muffins,
halved horizontally

1 tbsp butter

4 slices processed cheese

METHOD

1.   Mix the minced turkey with the sausagemeat, breadcrumbs, sage and egg yolk and season with salt and pepper. Shape into four patties.

2. Heat the oil in a large frying pan and fry the patties for 4 minutes on each side or until cooked through. Keep warm in a low oven.

3.   Fry the eggs in the frying pan until the whites are set, but the yolks are still a little runny.

4. Meanwhile, toast the muffin halves and spread them with butter.

5. Top the muffin bases with cheese and positon a sausage patty and a fried egg on top of each one.

6. Season with black pepper, then add the muffin tops and serve immediately.

Raspberry smoothie bowl

SERVES: 1 | PREPARATION TIME: 10 MINUTES

INGREDIENTS

1 large banana, sliced

100 g / 3 ½ oz / ⅔ cup raspberries

200 g / 7 oz natural yogurt

1 tbsp honey

100 ml / 3 ½ fl. oz / ½ cup almond milk

½ kiwi, sliced

½ nectarine, peeled and sliced

1 tsp chia seeds

1 tsp desiccated coconut

1 tsp chopped almonds

mint leaves, to garnish

METHOD

1. Place the banana, raspberries, yogurt, honey and almond milk into a blender, reserving a few slices of banana and raspberries for the topping.

2. Blend for a couple of minutes until smooth.

3. Pour into a serving bowl.

4. Arrange the remaining ingredients on top of the smoothie bowl.

Baked bananas

SERVES: 2 | PREP TIME: 5 MINUTES | COOKING TIME: 15 MINUTES

•••••••••••••••••••••••••

INGREDIENTS

3 bananas, peeled

150 ml / 5 ½ fl. oz / ⅔ cup coconut milk

½ tsp ground cinnamon

½ tsp ground ginger

2 tbsp muscovado sugar

2 tbsp flaked (slivered) almonds

METHOD

1. Preheat the oven to 180°C (160° fan) / 355F / gas 4.

2. Arrange the bananas in a small baking dish and pour over the coconut milk.

3. Mix the spices with the brown sugar and sprinkle over the top then scatter over the flaked almonds.

4. Bake in the oven for 15 minutes or until the bananas are soft and the liquid has thickened.

Sweet French toast

SERVES: 2 | PREP TIME: 5 MINUTES | COOKING TIME: 4 MINUTES

INGREDIENTS

1 orange, zest finely grated
2 large eggs
75 ml / 2 ½ fl. oz / ⅓ cup milk
25 g butter
8 slices baguette
4 tbsp runny honey

METHOD

1. Whisk the orange zest into the eggs with the milk.

2. Heat the butter in a large frying pan until sizzling.

3. Dip the baguette slices in the egg mixture on both sides until evenly coated then fry them for 2 minutes on each side or until golden brown.

4. Divide the toast between two plates.

5. Drizzle the toasts with honey and serve immediately.

Crêpes with chocolate dipping sauce

SERVES: 4 | PREP TIME: 5 MINUTES | COOKING TIME: 20 MINUTES

INGREDIENTS

150 g / 5 ½ oz / 1 cup plain (all-purpose) flour
1 large egg
325 ml / 11 ½ fl. oz / 1 ⅓ cups whole milk
30 g butter, melted

FOR THE DIPPING SAUCE:

100 ml / 3 ½ fl. oz / ½ cup double cream
1 tbsp brandy
100 g / 3 ½ oz / ¾ cup dark chocolate
(min. 60 % cocoa solids), chopped

METHOD

1. To make the dipping sauce, heat the cream and brandy to simmering point then pour it over the chocolate and stir to emulsify. Spoon into four serving glasses.

2. Sieve the flour into a bowl and make a well in the centre. Break in the egg and pour in the milk then use a whisk to gradually incorporate all of the flour from round the outside.

3. Melt the butter in a small frying pan then whisk it into the batter.

4. Put the buttered frying pan back over a low heat. Add a small ladle of batter and swirl the pan to coat the bottom.

5. When it starts to dry and curl up at the edges, turn the pancake over with a spatula and cook the other side until golden brown and cooked through.

6. Repeat with the rest of the mixture then fold the crêpes into quarters and serve with the dipping sauce.

Cook's Corner

Quick & Easy

Main meals

Chicken and chorizo paella

SERVES: 4-6 | PREP TIME: 5 MINUTES | COOKING TIME: 20 MINUTES

INGREDIENTS

1 tbsp olive oil

1 onion, diced

2 cloves of garlic,

200 g / 7 oz chorizo, sliced

400 g / 14 oz chicken, diced

1 tsp smoked paprika

a pinch of saffron

300 g / 10 ½ oz / 1 ½ cups paella rice

1 l / 34 fl. oz / 4 cups chicken stock, hot

150 g / 5 ¼ oz / 1 cup frozen peas

a small bunch of flat-leaved parsley

1 lemon, cut into wedges

METHOD

1. Heat the oil in a wide heavy bottomed pan. Add the onion and fry for 2–3 minutes until starting to turn translucent. Add the garlic and fry for a further minute.

2. Add the chorizo and chicken to the pan and brown for a couple of minutes.

3. Stir in the paprika, saffron and rice before adding the stock. Leave to cook for 12–15 minutes until the rice has absorbed the liquid and has softened. Add the peas to the pan after 5 minutes.

4. Stir through the parsley, season with salt and black pepper, and spoon onto serving plates with a wedge of lemon.

Broccoli gratin

SERVES: 1 | PREP TIME: 5 MINUTES | COOKING TIME: 15 MINUTES

INGREDIENTS

1 small head of broccoli, florets only

2 tbsp butter

1 clove of garlic, finely chopped

1 tbsp plain (all purpose) flour

150 ml / 5 ¼ fl. oz / ⅔ cup milk

100 g / 3 ½ oz / 1 cup Cheddar cheese, grated

a handful of flat-leaved parsley, chopped

1 lemon, juiced

salt and freshly ground black pepper

METHOD

1. Preheat the oven to 200°C (180°C fan) / 400F / gas 6.

2. Place the broccoli into a pan of salted boiling water and cook for 5 minutes until softened. Drain and place into an ovenproof dish.

3. Heat the butter in a saucepan until starting to foam. Add the garlic and cook for 1-2 minutes until fragrant. Stir in the flour and mix to form a roux leaving on the heat for a further minute, stirring all the time. Remove from the heat and whisk through the milk before returning to the heat. Whisk for 2–3 minutes until thickened.

4. Add three quarters of the cheese to the sauce and mix through until melted. Add the parsley, lemon juice and season with salt and black pepper.

5. Pour the sauce over the broccoli and top with the remaining cheese. Bake in the oven for 10 minutes until the cheese has melted and started to brown.

Pepperoni pizza

SERVES: 1-2 | PREP TIME: 5 MINUTES | COOKING TIME: 15 MINUTES

INGREDIENTS

1 pizza base

100 g / 3 ½ oz tomato passata

1 tsp dried oregano

1 tsp chilli (chili) flakes

1 tsp garlic powder

100 g / 3 ½ oz / 1 cup Cheddar cheese, grated

50 g / 1 ¾ oz pepperoni, sliced

METHOD

1. Preheat the oven to 220°C (200°C fan) / 425F / gas 7.

2. Place the pizza base onto a baking tray and ladle over the tomato passata. Spread over the base of the pizza using the bottom of the ladle.

3. Sprinkle over the oregano, chilli flakes and garlic powder so that it is evenly distributed.

4. Place the cheese over the tomato base and top with the sliced pepperoni.

5. Place into the hot oven for 12–15 minutes until crisp and the cheese has melted.

6. Serve with a drizzle of oil and freshly ground black pepper as desired.

Macaroni with fresh tomato sauce

SERVES: 2 | PREP TIME: 5 MINUTES | COOKING TIME: 12 MINUTES

INGREDIENTS

200 g / 7 oz / 2 cups macaroni pasta

2 medium tomatoes

2 tbsp fresh basil leaves, shredded

6 tbsp extra virgin olive oil

METHOD

1. Cook the macaroni in boiling salted water according to the packet instructions or until al dente.

2. While the pasta is cooking, score a cross in the top of each tomato and add them to the pasta water. When the skin of the tomatoes starts to curl up, remove them with a slotted spoon and dunk in a bowl of cold water.

3. Peel off and discard the skins then chop the tomato flesh into small cubes.

4. Mix the tomato in a bowl with the basil and olive oil and season well with salt and freshly ground black pepper.

5. Drain the pasta and return it to the saucepan, then stir in the tomato dressing. Put the pan back over the heat for 1 minute to warm through before serving.

Quinoa with cauliflower and eggs

SERVES: 2 | PREP TIME: 5 MINUTES | COOKING TIME: 15 MINUTES

INGREDIENTS

½ head cauliflower, florets chopped

2 tbsp olive oil

1 clove of garlic, minced

½ tsp turmeric

100 g / 3 ½ oz. / ½ cup quinoa

2 eggs

½ red onion, finely chopped

1 lemon, juice

A handful of flat leaf parsley, chopped

Salt and freshly ground black pepper

METHOD

1. Preheat the oven to 200°C (180°C fan) / 400F / gas 6.

2. Toss together the cauliflower florets, half the oil, turmeric and season. Roast in the oven for 12–15 minutes until browned.

3. Cook the quinoa as per the packet instructions, drain and spread onto a baking tray to cool.

4. Place the eggs into a pan of water and heat until boiling. Cook for 5 minutes, drain and once cool enough to handle peel off the shell and slice in half.

5. Combine the quinoa, cauliflower, onion, lemon juice, parsley and remaining oil. Mix to combine and season with salt and black pepper.

6. Divide between serving plates and top with the egg.

Pancetta and sun-dried tomato pizza

SERVES: 2 | PREP TIME: 2 MINUTES | COOKING TIME: 12 MINUTES

INGREDIENTS

1 large pizza base

3 tbsp crème fraîche

100 g / 3 ½ oz / 1 cup mozzarella, sliced

50 g / 1 ¾ oz / ⅓ cup pancetta, thinly sliced

3 tbsp sun-dried tomatoes in oil, drained

2 tbsp black olives, pitted and sliced

1 tbsp fresh thyme leaves

METHOD

1. Preheat the oven to 220°C (200° fan) / 430F / gas 7 and put a baking tray in to heat.

2. Spread the pizza base thinly with crème fraîche and arrange the mozzarella on top.

3. Lay the pancetta slices on top and scatter over the olives and thyme.

4. Give the top a good grind of black pepper then bake for 10 minutes or until the toppings are bubbling.

Lamb chops with garlic and rosemary

SERVES: 2 | PREP TIME: 5 MINUTES | COOKING TIME: 25 MINUTES

INGREDIENTS

6 lamb chops
1 bulb of garlic, separated into cloves
a few sprigs of rosemary
2 tbsp olive oil
2 slices lemon

METHOD

1. Preheat the oven to 200°C (180° fan) / 390F / gas 6.

2. Massage the lamb, garlic and rosemary with the olive oil and arrange in a roasting tin.

3. Season well with salt and pepper then bake for 25 minutes, turning the lamb chops over half way through.

4. Split the lamb and garlic between two plates and garnish with a slice of lemon.

Chicken fricassee

SERVES: 2-4 | PREP TIME: 5 MINUTES | COOKING TIME: 15 MINUTES

INGREDIENTS

150 g / 5 ¼ oz / ¾ cup easy cook rice

75 g / 2 ½ oz / ½ cup frozen peas

2 tbsp butter

400 g / 14 oz chicken breast fillets, cut into strips

1 onion, diced

100 g / 3 ½ oz. chestnut mushrooms, diced

1 clove garlic, minced

1 sprig thyme

150 ml / 5 ¼ fl. oz / ⅔ cup white wine

150 ml / 5 ¼ fl. oz / ⅔ cup chicken stock

150 ml / 5 ¼ fl. oz / ⅔ cup double (heavy) cream

a small bunch of flat-leaved parsley, chopped

a pinch of nutmeg

salt and freshly ground black pepper

METHOD

1. Cook the rice as per the packet instructions, drain and set aside.

2. Cook the peas in a pan of boiling water for 2-3 minutes, drain and set aside.

3. Heat the butter in a frying pan over a medium heat. Add the chicken and fry for 2-3 minutes until browned. Remove from the pan and set aside.

4. Add the onion and cook for 2-3 minutes until softened. Add the mushrooms, garlic and thyme to the pan and cook for a further 2–3 minutes until fragrant. Return the chicken to the pan.

5. Turn up the heat and add the wine, allow to bubble for a couple of minutes until the alcohol has cooked off. Pour the stock into the pan and leave for 5 minutes until thickened.

6. Remove from the heat and add the peas, cream, parsley, nutmeg and season to taste. Stir through to combine all the ingredients.

7. Serve the rice and chicken in serving bowls.

Cheeseburger with sausage meat

SERVES: 2 | PREP TIME: 5 MINUTES | COOKING TIME: 15 MINUTES

INGREDIENTS

2 100% beef burgers

100 g / 3 ½ oz sausage meat

2 carrots, shredded

1 tsp olive oil

1 tsp white wine vinegar

salt and freshly ground black pepper

2 cheese slices

2 burger buns

METHOD

1. Heat up a non-stick frying pan over a medium high heat. Add the burgers and cook for 6–7 minutes on each side.

2. As the burger cook add the sausage meat to the pan and fry for 8–10 minutes until starting to crisp.

3. Mix the carrots, oil and vinegar together in a bowl. Season with salt and black pepper and leave while the meat is cooking.

4. Place the cheese slices on top of the burgers once flipped to melt.

5. Cut the burger buns in half and top with the cooked burger followed by the crisped sausage meat. Top this with the shredded carrot before replacing the top of the bun.

Penne with smoked trout

SERVES: 4 | PREP TIME: 5 MINUTES | COOKING TIME: 30 MINUTES

INGREDIENTS

400 g / 14 oz / 4 cups penne
300 ml / 10 ½ oz / 1 ¼ cups crème fraîche
150 g / 5 ½ oz / 1 cup smoked trout, chopped
50 g / 1 ¾ oz / 2 cups watercress
50 g / 1 ¾ oz / ½ cup Emmental, grated

METHOD

1. Preheat the oven to 220°C (200° fan) / 430F / gas 7.

2. Cook the penne in boiling salted water according to the packet instructions or until al dente. Drain well.

3. Mix the crème fraîche with the trout and watercress then stir in the pasta and season with salt and pepper.

4. Spoon it into a baking dish and sprinkle with Emmental then bake for 15 minutes or until the top is golden.

Pepperoni and green pepper pizza

SERVES: 2 | PREP TIME: 2 MINUTES | COOKING TIME: 12 MINUTES

INGREDIENTS

1 large pizza base

3 tbsp passata sauce

100 g / 3 ½ oz / 1 cup mozzarella, sliced

100 g / 3 ½ oz / ⅔ cup pepperoni, sliced

½ green pepper, sliced

a few sprigs mint

METHOD

1. Preheat the oven to 220°C (200° fan) / 430F / gas 7 and put a baking tray in to heat.

2. Spread the pizza base thinly with passata and arrange the mozzarella slices on top.

3. Scatter over the pepperoni and green pepper and sprinkle with black pepper.

4. Bake the pizza for 10 minutes or until the toppings are bubbling.

5. Garnish with mint and serve immediately.

Stewed cabbage

SERVES: 2-4 | PREP TIME: 5 MINUTES | COOKING TIME: 20 MINUTES

INGREDIENTS

2 tbsp butter

1 onion, sliced

100 g / 3 ½ oz smoked bacon lardons

½ white cabbage, shredded

300 g / 10 ½ oz sauerkraut

2 bay leaves

150 g / 5 ¼ oz Polish kabanos sausage, sliced

300 ml / 10 fl. oz / 1 ¼ cups beef stock

salt and freshly ground black pepper

METHOD

1. Heat the butter in a large casserole pan with a lid. Add the onion and cook for 3-5 minutes until softened. Add the bacon lardons to the pan and cook for 2–3 minutes.

2. Add the white cabbage to the pan and stir through the juices in the pan, cook for 2–3 minutes until softened before adding the sauerkraut, bay leaves, kabanos and stock.

3. Cook for 8–10 minutes until the vegetables have softened and the sauce has thickened. Season with salt and black pepper to taste.

4. Spoon into warmed serving bowls and serve with crusty bread to soak up the juices.

Spaghetti with garlic and rosemary

SERVES: 2 | PREP TIME: 2 MINUTES | COOKING TIME: 12 MINUTES

INGREDIENTS

200 g / 7 oz / 2 cups spaghetti
4 tbsp olive oil
3 cloves garlic, crushed
2 tbsp fresh rosemary
2 tbsp Parmesan, freshly grated

METHOD

1. Cook the spaghetti in boiling salted water according to the packet instructions or until al dente.

2. Heat the oil in a sauté pan and stir-fry the garlic and rosemary for 2 minutes.

3. Reserve a couple of ladles of pasta water and drain the rest.

4. Stir the pasta into the garlic pan with 3 tablespoons of the pasta water and shake to emulsify with the oil. If it looks a bit dry, add some more pasta water.

5. Divide between two warm bowls and sprinkle over the Parmesan.

Rigatoni with meatballs

SERVES: 4 | PREP TIME: 10 MINUTES | COOKING TIME: 15 MINUTES

INGREDIENTS

6 good quality sausages, skinned

400 g / 14 oz / 4 cups rigatoni pasta

4 tbsp olive oil

2 cloves garlic, crushed

300 ml / 10 ½ fl. oz / 1 ½ cups tomato passata

50 g / 1 ¾ oz / ½ cup Parmesan, finely grated

4 tbsp breadcrumbs

METHOD

1. Roll the sausagemeat into small round or flattened meatballs.

2. Cook the rigatoni in boiling salted water according to the packet instructions.

3. Meanwhile, heat the oil in a frying pan and fry the meatballs for 6 minutes or until golden on all sides.

4. Add the garlic to the pan and cook for 1 minute, then pour in the passata and a sprinkle of salt and pepper and simmer for 5 minutes.

5. Drain the pasta and stir it into the frying pan. Let it absorb some of the sauce for a minute then spoon it into four oven-proof bowls.

6. Sprinkle liberally with Parmesan and breadcrumbs, put under the grill for 2 minutes then serve.

Stir-fried chilli squid

SERVES: 4 | PREP TIME: 2 MINUTES | COOKING TIME: 4 MINUTES

INGREDIENTS

2 tbsp olive oil

2 cloves garlic, finely chopped

2 red chillies, thinly sliced

1 tsp red chilli flakes

300 g / 10 ½ oz / 2 cups raw squid rings

½ lemon, juiced

2 tsp lemon zest

1 tsp sprigs parsley, to serve

METHOD

1. Heat 1 tablespoon of oil in a large wok and fry the garlic, thinly sliced chillies and chilli flakes for 30 seconds.

2. Add the squid rings and cook for 1 minute or until they just turn opaque then stir in the spinach, lemon juice and lemon zest.

3. Place the squid onto a long serving plate and sprinkle over the sprigs of parsley.

4. Serve immediately.

Farfalle with peppers, feta and lemon

SERVES: 4 | PREP TIME: 2 MINUTES | COOKING TIME: 12 MINUTES

INGREDIENTS

400 g / 14 oz / 5 cups farfalle pasta

4 tbsp olive oil

4 cloves garlic, crushed

2 yellow peppers, thinly sliced

1 small preserved lemon, quartered and thinly sliced

100 g / 3 ½ oz / ⅔ cup feta, cubed

a small bunch of basil, leaves only

METHOD

1. Cook the farfalle in boiling salted water according to the packet instructions or until al dente.

2. While the pasta is cooking, heat the olive oil in a large frying pan and cook the garlic and peppers for 8 minutes, stirring occasionally.

3. Reserve 1 ladle of the pasta water and drain the rest then stir the pasta into the peppers with the preserved lemon and feta. Add a little of the cooking water if it looks too dry.

4. Chop half the basil and stir it into the pan, reserving the rest for garnish.

5. Divide the pasta between four warm bowls and scatter over the basil leaves.

Baked polenta

SERVES: 2 | PREP TIME: 5 MINUTES | COOKING TIME: 15 MINUTES

INGREDIENTS

200 ml / 7 fl. oz / ¾ cup water
120 ml / 4 fl. oz / ½ cup milk
1 tbsp butter
100 g / 3 ½ oz / ½ cup quick cook polenta
50 g / 1 ¾ oz / ½ cup parmesan cheese, grated
75 g / 2 ½ oz tomato passata
125 g / 4 ¼ oz buffalo mozzarella, sliced
1 tsp dried basil
1 tsp dried oregano
2 tbsp olive oil
salt and freshly ground black pepper
flat-leaved parsley, to garnish

METHOD

1. Preheat the oven to 220°C (200°C fan) / 425F / gas 7 and lightly grease an ovenproof dish.

2. Place the water, milk and butter into a saucepan and heat until boiling. Pour the polenta into the pan and mix continuously until thickened, around 3–4 minutes.

3. Mix the parmesan through the polenta and season to taste. Pour into the prepared ovenproof dish and pour the passata over the top. Add the sliced mozzarella and herbs before baking in the oven to 10–12 minutes until the cheese has melted.

4. Remove from the oven and drizzle over the olive oil and season with salt and black pepper. Garnish with the parsley then serve.

Beetroot and tomato soup

SERVES: 4 | PREP TIME: 5 MINUTES | COOKING TIME: 20 MINUTES

INGREDIENTS

2 tbsp olive oil

1 onion, finely chopped

2 cloves garlic, crushed

200 g / 7 oz / 2 cups canned tomatoes, chopped

250 g / 9 oz / 1 cup cooked beetroot, cubed

500 ml / 18 fl. oz / 2 cups vegetable stock

METHOD

1. Heat the oil in a saucepan and fry the onion for 5 minutes or until softened. Add the garlic and cook for 2 more minutes then stir in the tomatoes and beetroot.

2. Pour in the vegetable stock and bring to the boil.

3. Simmer for 10 minutes then blend until smooth with an immersion blender.

4. Try the soup and adjust the seasoning with salt and pepper.

5. Ladle into warm bowls and serve immediately.

Quinoa and broccoli salad

SERVES: 2 | PREP TIME: 5 MINUTES | COOKING TIME: 15 MINUTES

INGREDIENTS

100 g / 3 ½ oz / ½ cup quinoa

1 small head of broccoli, florets only

1 lemon, juiced

2 tbsp olive oil

½ red onion, finely chopped

100 g / 3 ½ oz / ½ cup pomegranate seeds

METHOD

1. Cook the quinoa as per the packet instructions. Once drained, spread over a baking tray to cool quickly.

2. Place the broccoli into a pan of salted boiling water and cook for 5–6 minutes until tender. Drain well and set aside.

3. Mix the cooked quinoa with the lemon juice and olive oil before seasoning with salt and black pepper.

4. Divide the quinoa and broccoli between two serving plates and top with the red onion and pomegranate seeds.

Salmon with spring onions

SERVES: 2 | PREP TIME: 5 MINUTES | COOKING TIME: 6 MINUTES

INGREDIENTS

1 egg white, beaten

1 tbsp cornflour

2 portions salmon fillet, skinned

50 g / 1 ¾ oz / ⅓ cup spring onions (scallions),
finely chopped

2 tbsp olive oil

METHOD

1. Mix the egg white with the cornflour and brush
   a thin layer onto the skinned side of the salmon.
   Dip the salmon in the chopped spring onions,
   pressing down firmly so they stick in an
   even layer.

2. Heat half the oil in a large frying pan and cook
   the salmon, spring onion side down, for 4 minutes.

3. Turn the salmon over, turn off the heat and let
   the other side cook in the residual heat of the
   pan for 2 minutes. If any spring onions have
   fallen off the salmon, place them back on top.
   Season to taste.

4. Serve the salmon spring onion side up with a
   small side salad.

Pasta with spring onion and chickpeas

SERVES: 4 | PREP TIME: 5 MINUTES | COOKING TIME: 12 MINUTES

INGREDIENTS

400 g / 14 oz / 4 cups farfalle pasta

8 spring onions (scallions)

4 tbsp olive oil

200 g / 7 oz / 1 ½ cups canned chickpeas, drained

4 tbsp pesto

100 g / 3 ½ oz / ⅔ cup goat's cheese

METHOD

1. Cook the farfalle in boiling salted water.

2. Meanwhile, chop the spring onions. Thinly slice the white part lengthways then fry in the oil for 8 minutes or until starting to caramelise.

3. Two minutes before the pasta is ready, add the chickpeas to the pasta pan to warm through. Drain and toss with the pesto.

4. Divide between four plates and crumble over the goat's cheese, then top with the caramelised spring onions and their oil and the chopped spring onion tops.

Beef with ginger, peppers and tomato

SERVES: 4 | PREP TIME: 5 MINUTES | COOKING TIME: 8 MINUTES

INGREDIENTS

3 tbsp vegetable oil
2 cloves garlic, thinly sliced
1 tbsp root ginger, sliced
300 g / 10 ½ oz / 2 cups sirloin steak, cubed
1 red pepper, julienned
100 g / 3 ½ oz / ¾ cup cherry tomatoes, halved
2 tbsp rice wine or dry sherry
1 tsp caster (superfine) sugar
1 tbsp light soy sauce
coriander (cilantro) leaves to garnish

METHOD

1. Heat the oil in a large wok and fry the garlic and ginger for 30 seconds.

2. Add the steak, peppers and tomatoes and stir-fry for 4 minutes or until the beef is cooked through.

3. Mix the rice wine, sugar and soy together and add it to the wok.

4. Stir-fry for 2 more minutes then serve immediately, garnished with coriander.

Chicken, honey and sesame stir-fry

SERVES: 4 | PREP TIME: 5 MINUTES | COOKING TIME: 8 MINUTES

INGREDIENTS

3 tbsp vegetable oil
2 cloves garlic, finely chopped
1 tbsp root ginger, finely chopped
225 g / 7 oz / 1 ½ cups chicken breast, cubed
2 tbsp sesame seeds
1 carrot, thinly sliced lengthways
100 g / 3 ½ oz / 1 cup sugar snap peas, trimmed
100 g / 3 ½ oz / ¾ cup baby sweetcorn
8 spring onions (scallions), trimmed
2 tbsp rice wine or dry sherry
2 tbsp runny honey
1 tbsp light soy sauce
100 g / 3 ½ oz / 1 cup canned white
asparagus, drained

METHOD

1. Heat the oil in a large wok and fry the garlic and ginger for 30 seconds.

2. Add the chicken and sesame seeds and stir-fry for 2 minutes then add the carrot, sugar snaps, sweetcorn and spring onions and stir-fry for another 2 minutes.

3. Mix the rice wine with the honey and soy and add it to the wok with the asparagus.

4. Stir-fry for 2 more minutes then serve immediately.

Fish fingers

SERVES: 4 | PREP TIME: 15 MINUTES | COOKING TIME: 4-5 MINUTES

INGREDIENTS

800 g / 1 lb 12 oz / 4 cups line-caught pollock fillet

4 tbsp plain (all-purpose) flour

1 egg, beaten

75 g / 2 ½ oz / ½ cup panko breadcrumbs

2–3 litres / 3 ½ pints–5 pints / 8–12 cups
sunflower oil

METHOD

1. Cut the fish into 16 evenly sized fingers.

2. Put the flour, egg and panko breadcrumbs in three separate bowls. Dip the fish fingers first in the flour, then in the egg, then the breadcrumbs.

3. Heat the oil in a deep fat fryer, according to the manufacturer's instructions, to 180°C.

4. Lower the fish fingers in the fryer basket and cook for 4–5 minutes or until crisp and golden brown. You may need to cook them in two batches to avoid overcrowding the fryer, in which case keep the first batch warm in a low oven.

5. Line a large bowl with a thick layer of kitchen paper and when they are ready, tip them into the bowl to remove any excess oil.

6. Sprinkle with sea salt to taste.

Stir-fried turkey with peppers

SERVES: 4 | PREP TIME: 5 MINUTES | COOKING TIME: 8 MINUTES

INGREDIENTS

3 tbsp vegetable oil

2 cloves garlic, finely chopped

1 tbsp root ginger, finely chopped

300 g / 10 ½ oz / 1 ¾ cup turkey breast, cubed

1 red pepper, julienned

1 yellow pepper, julienned

1 green pepper, julienned

2 tbsp rice wine or dry sherry

1 tsp caster (superfine) sugar

1 tbsp light soy sauce

METHOD

1. Heat the oil in a large wok and fry the garlic and ginger for 30 seconds.

2. Add the turkey and peppers and stir-fry for 4 minutes or until the turkey is cooked through.

3. Mix the rice wine, sugar and soy together and add it to the wok.

4. Stir-fry for 2 more minutes then serve immediately.

Broccoli and bacon salad

SERVES: 2 | PREP TIME: 10 MINUTES | COOKING TIME: 10 MINUTES

INGREDIENTS

3 tbsp olive oil

4 rashers streaky bacon

1 small head broccoli, broken into small florets

1 tsp runny honey

1 tsp Dijon mustard

1 tbsp balsamic vinegar

30 g Parmesan

METHOD

1. Heat 1 tablespoon of the oil in a frying pan and fry the bacon for 3 minutes on each side or until crisp.

2. Meanwhile, blanch the broccoli in boiling salted water for 3–4 minutes or until just tender. Drain well.

3. While the bacon and broccoli are cooking, whisk the honey and mustard into the vinegar with a pinch of salt then incorporate the rest of the oil.

4. Toss the drained broccoli with the dressing and split between two serving plates.

5. Lay 2 rashers of bacon on top of each plate and use a vegetable peeler to shave over some Parmesan.

Beef stew

SERVES: 1 | PREP TIME: 5 MINUTES | COOKING TIME: 15 MINUTES

INGREDIENTS

2 tbsp olive oil

200 g / 7 oz beef rump steak

1 tbsp flour

1 onion, roughly chopped

1 carrot, sliced

1 potato, cubed

2 sprigs of thyme

250 ml / 8 ½ fl. oz / 1 cup beef stock

salt and freshly ground black pepper

METHOD

1. Heat the oil in a heavy bottomed casserole pan over a high heat and add the steak. Cook for 2 minutes on each side and remove. Chop the steak and mix with the flour.

2. Add the onion, carrot, potato and thyme to the pan and fry for 3–5 minutes until starting to brown at the edges.

3. Pour the stock into the pan and simmer for 10 minutes until the vegetables have softened.

4. Return the meat to the pan and stir through for a minute until the sauce has thickened. Season with salt and black pepper to taste.

Salmon with peppers and tartare sauce

SERVES: 2 | PREP TIME: 4 MINUTES | COOKING TIME: 6 MINUTES

INGREDIENTS

2 portions salmon fillet
2 tbsp olive oil
1 jar roasted pepper in oil, drained
1 tbsp walnuts, chopped
1 tbsp fresh dill, chopped

FOR THE TARTARE SAUCE:
3 tbsp mayonnaise
2 gherkins, finely chopped
1 tsp baby capers
½ shallot, finely chopped
2 tsp lemon juice

METHOD

1. Preheat a frying pan until smoking hot.

2. Brush the salmon fillets with the oil and season with salt and pepper.

3. Fry the salmon for 3 minutes on each side.

4. Meanwhile, mix the peppers with the walnuts and dill and season to taste.

5. To make the tartare sauce, stir the ingredients together with a little freshly ground black pepper.

6. Serve the salmon on a bed of red peppers with a spoonful of tartar sauce on the side.

Stir-fried prawns and pineapple

SERVES: 2 | PREP TIME: 5 MINUTES | COOKING TIME: 5 MINUTES

••••••••••••••••••••••••••••

INGREDIENTS

3 tbsp vegetable oil

2 cloves of garlic, thinly sliced

1 tbsp root ginger, thinly sliced

200 g / 7 oz / 1 cup raw prawns (shrimp), peeled with tails left intact

300 g / 10 ½ oz / 1 ½ cups canned pineapple rings, drained and halved

2 tbsp rice wine or dry sherry

1 tsp caster (superfine) sugar

1 tbsp light soy sauce

a small bunch of chives, cut into short lengths

METHOD

1. Heat the oil in a large wok and fry the garlic and ginger for 30 seconds.

2. Add the prawns and pineapple and stir-fry for 2 minutes or until the prawns turn opaque.

3. Mix the rice wine, sugar and soy together and add it to the wok.

4. Stir-fry for 2 more minutes then serve immediately, garnished with chives.

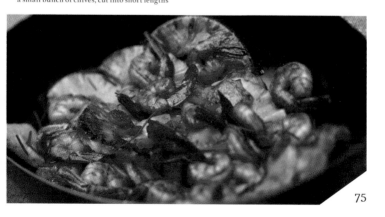

Mustard chicken

SERVES: 4 | PREP TIME: 5 MINUTES | COOKING TIME: 10 MINUTES

INGREDIENTS

2 tbsp grain mustard

1 tbsp olive oil

1 tsp rosemary, finely chopped

4 chicken breasts

METHOD

1. Preheat the grill to its highest setting.

2. Grill the chicken for 5 minutes on each side or until fully cooked through.

3. Mix together the mustard, oil and rosemary with a pinch of salt and pepper.

4. Once the chicken is cooked, pour the mustard mixture over each chicken breast and serve immediately, with potato wedges or salad.

Sautéed potatoes, courgettes and feta

SERVES: 2 | PREP TIME: 2 MINUTES | COOKING TIME: 25 MINUTES

INGREDIENTS

6 tbsp olive oil

400 g / 14 oz / 2 ⅔ cup charlotte potatoes, peeled and cubed

1 courgette (zucchini), halved and thinly sliced

100 g / 3 ½ oz / ⅔ cup feta, cubed

a small bunch chives, chopped

METHOD

1. Boil the potatoes in salted water for 8 minutes then drain well and leave to steam dry for 2 minutes.

2. Heat 4 tablespoons of the oil in a large pan.

3. Season the potatoes with plenty of salt and pepper then fry for 10 minutes, shaking the pan and stirring occasionally.

4. Add the courgette slices and stir-fry for 2 more minutes then stir in the feta and chives and serve immediately.

Gnocchetti with cherry tomatoes

SERVES: 4 | PREP TIME: 5 MINUTES | COOKING TIME: 20 MINUTES

INGREDIENTS

300 g / 10 oz / 1 ¼ cups cherry tomatoes

1 tbsp olive oil

500 g / 1 lb / 2 cups gnocchetti pasta

handful basil

2 tbsp Parmesan, grated to serve

METHOD

1. Preheat the oven to 200°C (180° fan) / 400 F / gas 6.

2. Place the cherry tomatoes in a roasting tin and drizzle with oil. Season and roast in the oven for at least 20 minutes or until starting to blacken.

3. Meanwhile cook the pasta in boiling salted water according to packet instructions

4. Drain the pasta.

5. Toss the pasta with the tomatoes and their roasting juices and chopped basil.

6. Adjust the seasoning and serve with Parmesan.

Stir-fried salmon with vegetables

SERVES: 4 | PREP TIME: 5 MINUTES | COOKING TIME: 8 MINUTES

INGREDIENTS

3 tbsp vegetable oil
2 cloves garlic, finely chopped
1 tbsp root ginger, finely chopped
150 g / 5 ½ oz / 1 cup baby carrots, peeled
150 g / 5 ½ oz / 1 ½ cups asparagus spears
300 g / 10 ½ oz / 2 cups salmon fillet, cubed
1 red pepper, julienned
1 yellow pepper, julienned
1 green pepper, julienned
2 tbsp rice wine or dry sherry
1 tsp caster (superfine) sugar
1 tbsp light soy sauce
1 tbsp sesame seeds

METHOD

1. Heat the oil in a large wok and fry the garlic and ginger for 30 seconds.

2. Add the carrots and asparagus and stir-fry for 2 minutes then add the salmon and peppers and stir-fry for another 2 minutes.

3. Mix the rice wine, sugar and soy together and add it to the wok with the sesame seeds.

4. Stir-fry for 2 more minutes then serve immediately.

Roast chicken with vegetables

SERVES: 1 | PREP TIME: 5 MINUTES | COOKING TIME: 20 MINUTES

INGREDIENTS

1 chicken breast with skin
1 tbsp olive oil
salt and freshly ground black pepper
½ head of broccoli, florets only
75 g / 2 ½ oz / ½ cup garden peas
1 egg

METHOD

1. Preheat the oven to 200°C (180°C fan) / 400F / gas 6.

2. Place the chicken onto a baking tray and rub with half the oil before seasoning.

3. Place the chicken into the oven and roast for 18-20 minutes until the skin is crisp and the juices run clear when pierced with a knife.

4. Add the broccoli to a pan of salted boiling water and cook for 5–6 minutes. Add the peas to the broccoli pan for the last 2 minutes.

5. Heat the remaining oil in a non-stick frying pan and fry the egg for 3–4 minutes.

6. Slice the roast chicken and place onto a plate with the drained vegetables and fried egg. Season with salt and black pepper and serve with lemon wedges if desired.

Salmon mimosa salad

SERVES: 1 | PREP TIME: 15 MINUTES | COOKING TIME: 5 MINUTES

INGREDIENTS

3 eggs

50 g / 1 ¾ oz boiled potatoes, grated

2 carrots, grated

100 g / 3 ½ oz canned salmon, drained

50 g / 1 ¾ oz mayonnaise

2 tsp fresh dill, chopped

salt and freshly ground black pepper

METHOD

1. Place the eggs into a pan of water, heat until boiling and cook for 5 minutes until hard boiled. Drain and set aside to cool enough to handle.

2. Once cooled, peel and separate the white from the yolk.

3. Place a ring mould onto a serving plate.

4. Spoon alternate layers of potatoes, carrots, egg whites and salmon into the ring. Seasoning with salt and pepper and a spoonful of mayonnaise mixed with the dill.

5. Top the stack with the reserved egg yolks by crumbling them over the top.

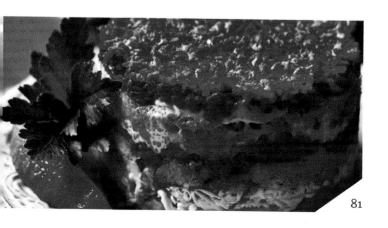

Guacamole tacos

SERVES: 4 | PREPARATION TIME: 4 MINUTES

• •

INGREDIENTS

4 ripe avocados

1 red onion, finely chopped

1 red chilli, finely chopped

3 medium tomatoes, diced

2 tbsp coriander leaves, chopped

2 limes, juiced

TO SERVE:

8 corn tacos

METHOD

1. Mash the avocados with a fork then stir in the rest of the guacamole ingredients. Season to taste with salt and white pepper.

2. Divide the guacamole between 8 tacos and serve 2 tacos per person.

Beef and parsley burgers

SERVES: 4 | PREP TIME: 10 MINUTES | COOKING TIME: 10-12 MINUTES

INGREDIENTS

450 g / 1 lb / 2 cups minced beef
2 salad onions, finely chopped
4 tbsp flat leaf parsley, chopped
1 tbsp baby capers
1 tsp Dijon mustard
2 tbsp olive oil

TO SERVE:
baby salad leaves
4 salad onions, halved
4 sprigs flat leaf parsley

METHOD

1. Put the mince in a bowl with the onion, parsley, capers and mustard, and knead with your hands until well mixed and starting to get sticky.

2. Divide the mixture into 4 and shape it into burgers, squeezing the patties firmly with your hands.

3. Heat the oil in a frying pan and cook the burgers for 10–12 minutes, turning every 2 minutes.

4. Serve the burgers on a bed of salad leaves, garnished with salad onions and parsley.

Avocado and spinach salad

SERVES: 1 | PREPARATION TIME: 5 MINUTES

INGREDIENTS

1 avocado

75 g / 2 ½ oz. baby spinach leaves

50 g / 1 ¾ oz. / ¼ cup pomegranate seeds

1 tbsp extra virgin olive oil

METHOD

1. Cut the avocado in half and remove the stone. Peel and then chop into slices.

2. Wash the spinach leaves and squeeze out any excess moisture.

3. Place the spinach and sliced avocado onto a serving plate.

4. Top with the pomegranate seeds and season with salt and black pepper and a drizzle of oil.

Handmade cheeseburger

SERVES: 2 | PREP TIME: 10 MINUTES | COOKING TIME: 10 MINUTES

INGREDIENTS

300 g / 10 ½ oz quality beef steak mince

1 tsp onion granules

1 tsp garlic powder

1 tsp dried parsley

sea salt and freshly ground black pepper

2 Cheddar cheese slices

2 burger buns

50 g / 1 ¾ oz rocket (arugula)

METHOD

1. Place the steak mince, onion granules, garlic powder, parsley and a generous amount of salt and black pepper into a mixing bowl. Using your hands, bring the mixture together before dividing into two equal sized portions. Shape into round burger patties.

2. Heat a griddle pan or non-stick frying pan until hot. Place the patties into the pan and cook for 5 minutes without moving them. Flip the burgers over and cook for a further 5 minutes, placing the cheese slices on top of the burgers.

3. Cut the buns in half and place them under a grill, only toast the cut side of the buns.

4. Place the buns onto serving plates and top with rocket. Place the burgers on top and replace the top half of the toasted bun.

Sole and mushroom skewers with rice

SERVES: 4 | PREP TIME: 20 MINUTES | COOKING TIME: 26 MINUTES

INGREDIENTS

200 g / 7 oz / 2 cups / 1 cup mixed basmati, red and wild rice

450 g / 1 lb / 3 cups sole, filleted and cut into strips

200 g / 7 oz / 2 cups / 2⅔ cups button mushrooms, halved

2 tbsp olive oil

fresh coriander (cilantro) sprigs to garnish

METHOD

1. Put 16 wooden skewers in a bowl of water and leave to soak for 20 minutes. Meanwhile, put the rice in a large saucepan and add enough water to cover it by 1 cm. Bring to the boil, then cover and turn down the heat to the lowest setting.

2. Cook for 10 minutes then turn off the heat and leave to stand for 10 minutes.

3. Preheat the grill to its highest setting. Roll up the sole fillets and thread them onto the skewers with the mushrooms. Brush the skewers with oil and spread them out on a large grill tray.

4. Sprinkle with salt and grill for 3 minutes on each side or until golden brown and cooked through.

Fried gnocchi with tomato sauce

SERVES: 4 | PREP TIME: 5 MINUTES | COOKING TIME: 20 MINUTES

INGREDIENTS

4 tbsp olive oil

500 g / 1 lb 2 oz / 2 cups ready-made gnocchi

FOR THE SAUCE:

4 tbsp olive oil

1 onion, sliced

2 cloves of garlic, crushed

400 g / 14 oz / 2 cups canned tomatoes, chopped

METHOD

1. Heat the oil in a sauté pan and fry the onion for 5 minutes to soften. Add the garlic and cook for 2 more minutes, then stir in the tomatoes. Simmer for 15 minutes.

2. Meanwhile, heat the oil in a large non-stick frying pan and fry the gnocchi for 5 minutes, turning once.

3. Divide the gnocchi between four warm bowls and top with a spoonful of tomato sauce.

Ricotta and olive pizza

SERVES: 2 | PREP TIME: 2 MINUTES | COOKING TIME: 12 MINUTES

INGREDIENTS

1 large pizza base

3 tbsp soft cheese with herbs

100 g / 3 ½ oz / 1 cup salted ricotta

2 tomatoes, thinly sliced

1 garlic clove, thinly sliced

50 g / 1 ¾ oz / ⅔ cup black olives, pitted and sliced

2 pinches thyme leaves

a handful of basil leaves

METHOD

1. Preheat the oven to 220°C (200° fan) / 430F / gas 7 and put a baking tray in to heat.

2. Spread the pizza base thinly with the soft cheese and crumble over the ricotta.

3. Arrange the slices of tomato on top then scatter over the olives, slices of garlic and thyme leaves.

4. Give the top a grind of black pepper then bake for 10 minutes or until the toppings are bubbling.

5. Scatter over the basil leaves and serve immediately.

Farfalle with salmon

SERVES: 1 | PREP TIME: 5 MINUTES | COOKING TIME: 15 MINUTES

INGREDIENTS

75 g / 2 ½ oz. farfalle

1 tsp olive oil

1 salmon fillet

125 ml / 4 ½ fl. oz / ½ cup white wine

150 ml / 5 ¼ fl. oz / ⅔ cup double (heavy) cream

2 tbsp parmesan cheese, grated

Salt and freshly ground black pepper

METHOD

1. Place the pasta into a pan of salted boiling water and cook for 10-12 minutes until softened. Drain and set aside.

2. As the pasta is cooking, heat the oil in a non-stick frying pan over a medium heat. Season the salmon and place skin side down in the pan. Fry for 6–8 minutes until the skin is crisp before turning over and cooking for a further 4-6 minutes. Remove from the pan and flake the flesh of the fish.

3. Pour the wine into the pan that you cooked the fish in. Allow to bubble and reduce for 2–3 minutes before adding the cream. Stir though until combined.

4. Return the fish to the sauce and add the drained pasta. Mix through and season with salt and black pepper to taste. Top with parmesan.

Tagliatelle with savoy cabbage and ham

SERVES: 2 | PREP TIME: 2 MINUTES | COOKING TIME: 14 MINUTES

INGREDIENTS

200 g / 7 oz / 2 cups / 2 cups tagliatelle

200 g / 7 oz / 2 cups / 2 cups Savoy cabbage, sliced

1 tbsp butter

1 tsp caraway seeds

1 tsp Dijon mustard

200 ml / 7 fl. oz / ¾ cup double cream

100 g / 3 ½ oz / ⅔ cup cooked ham, in strips

METHOD

1. Cook the tagliatelle in boiling salted water according to the packet instructions or until al dente.

2. 4 minutes before the end of cooking time, add the cabbage to the pan.

3. Meanwhile, melt the butter in a frying pan and cook the caraway seeds for 1 minute. Stir in the mustard and cream and ham.

4. Drain the pasta and cabbage and stir them into the cream. Cook for 2 minutes for the flavours to mingle then serve.

Farfalle with pepper and basil sauce

SERVES: 4 | PREP TIME: 2 MINUTES | COOKING TIME: 12 MINUTES

INGREDIENTS

400 g / 14 oz / 2 cups farfalle pasta
4 tbsp olive oil
4 cloves garlic, crushed
2 orange peppers, finely chopped
a small bunch of basil, leaves only

METHOD

1. Cook the farfalle in boiling salted water according to the packet instructions or until al dente.

2. While the pasta is cooking, heat the olive oil in a large frying pan and cook the garlic and peppers for 8 minutes, stirring occasionally.

3. Scrape the mixture into a food processor and blend to a smooth puree, then return it to the frying pan.

4. Drain the pasta and stir it into the pepper puree. Add the basil leaves and put the pan back over the heat for 1 minute to warm through before serving.

Potato and chorizo crustless quiche

SERVES: 4 | PREP TIME: 5 MINUTES | COOKING TIME: 20-25 MINUTES

INGREDIENTS

4 boiled potatoes, cooled and cubed

½ chorizo sausage, cubed

½ jar sun-dried tomatoes in oil, drained and chopped

2 tbsp olive oil

6 free-range eggs

pea shoots to garnish

METHOD

1. Preheat the oven to 180°C (160° fan) / 355F / gas 4.

2. Fry the potatoes and chorizo in the oil for 5 minutes then stir in the sun-dried tomatoes.

3. Lightly beat the eggs and stir in the chorizo and potatoes.

4. Pour the mixture into a non-stick cake tin and bake in the oven for 20 minutes or until just set in the centre.

5. Garnish with pea shoots and serve warm or at room temperature.

Penne with spicy tomato sauce

SERVES: 2 | PREP TIME: 2 MINUTES | COOKING TIME: 25 MINUTES

INGREDIENTS

4 tbsp olive oil

2 cloves of garlic, crushed

2 red chillies, finely chopped

1 tsp smoked paprika

100 g / 3 ½ oz / ½ cup canned tomatoes, chopped

200 g / 7 oz / 2 cups penne pasta

METHOD

1. Heat the oil in a frying pan and fry the garlic and chillies for 2 minutes.

2. Stir in the smoked paprika then add the canned tomatoes and simmer for 20 minutes.

3. Meanwhile, cook the penne in boiling salted water according to the packet instructions or until al dente.

4. Taste the sauce for seasoning, adding plenty of freshly ground black pepper.

5. Drain the pasta and stir it into the sauce then divide between two warm bowls and serve immediately.

Spicy chicken stew

SERVES: 2-4 | PREP TIME: 5 MINUTES | COOKING TIME: 20 MINUTES

INGREDIENTS

4 chicken thighs

2 tbsp olive oil

salt and freshly ground black pepper

1 onion, diced

2 cloves of garlic, chopped

2 red chillies (chilies), sliced

1 tsp paprika

1 tsp cayenne

400 g / 14 oz canned chopped tomatoes

small bunch of flat-leaved parsley, chopped

METHOD

1. Preheat the oven to 200°C (180°C fan) / 400F / gas 6.

2. Rub half the oil over the chicken thighs and season with salt and black pepper. Place into the oven and roast for 18-20 minutes or until the juices run clear when pierced with a sharp knife.

3. Heat the remaining oil in a sauté pan. Add the onions and cook for 5–6 minutes until softened. Add the garlic, chillies, paprika and cayenne and cook for a further minute until fragrant. Add the chopped tomatoes to the pan and cover, simmer for 12–15 minutes.

4. Remove the chicken from the oven and add to the pan with the tomato and onions. Mix through the sauce to coat.

5. Stir through the chopped parsley and season with taste before serving.

Pan-fried salmon with green salad

SERVES: 1 | PREP TIME: 5 MINUTES | COOKING TIME: 10 MINUTES

INGREDIENTS

1 tbsp olive oil

1 salmon fillet

½ lemon, juiced

100 g / 3 ½ oz lamb's lettuce

salt and freshly ground black pepper

METHOD

1. Heat half the oil in a non-stick frying pan over a medium heat. Season the salmon and place skin side down in the pan. Fry for 6-8 minutes until the skin is crisp before turning over and cooking for a further 4-6 minutes, squeezing over the lemon juice.

2. Place the salad leaves onto a serving plate and drizzle over the remaining oil and seasoning with salt and black pepper.

3. Place the salmon onto the plate and garnish with a wedge of lemon as desired.

Spaghetti with green beans

SERVES: 2 | PREP TIME: 2 MINUTES | COOKING TIME: 12 MINUTES

INGREDIENTS

200 g / 7 oz / 1 cup spaghetti

200 g / 7 oz green beans

4 tbsp olive oil

3 cloves garlic, crushed

2 tbsp flat leaf parsley, finely chopped

METHOD

1. Cook the spaghetti in boiling salted water according to the packet instructions or until al dente.

2. Meanwhile, blanch the green beans in boiling salted water for 3–4 minutes or until just tender. Drain well.

3. Heat the oil in a sauté pan and fry the garlic for 2 minutes. Add the drained beans and cook, stirring occasionally, for 3 minutes so they can take on the flavour from the oil. Season to taste with salt and pepper.

4. Reserve a couple of ladles of pasta water and drain the rest.

5. Stir the pasta into the green bean pan with 3 tablespoons of the pasta water and shake to emulsify with the oil. If it looks a bit dry, add some more pasta water.

6. Divide between two warm bowls and serve immediately.

Green chicken curry

SERVES: 2 | PREP TIME: 5 MINUTES | COOKING TIME: 15 MINUTES

INGREDIENTS

100 g / 3 ½ oz / ½ cup easy cook basmati rice

1 tbsp cooking oil

250 g / 9 oz chicken breast, diced

1 tbsp Thai green curry paste

400 ml / 13 ½ fl. oz / 1 ⅔ cups coconut milk

2 spring onions (scallions), chopped

1 lemon, cut into wedges

METHOD

1. Cook the rice as per the packet instructions, drain and set aside.

2. Heat the oil over a high heat in a wok or high sided pan. Once hot add the chicken and fry for 2-3 minutes until browned.

3. Add the curry paste and mix through the chicken for 1 minute until fragrant. Add a quarter of the coconut milk to loosen before pouring in the rest of the can. Leave to simmer for 10 minutes until hot and the chicken is cooked.

4. Serve the chicken curry with the rice. Garnish with the chopped spring onions and lemon wedges.

Pork and broccoli with mustard sauce

SERVES: 4 | PREP TIME: 2 MINUTES | COOKING TIME: 20 MINUTES

INGREDIENTS

2 tbsp olive oil

1 large onion, halved and sliced

2 garlic cloves, crushed

450 g / 1 lb / 3 cups pork fillet, thinly sliced

2 tsp Dijon mustard

1 tsp grain mustard

100 ml / 3 ½ fl. oz / ½ cup white wine

1 small head broccoli, broken into florets

400 ml / 14 fl. oz / 1 ⅔ cup double cream

½ lemon, juiced

METHOD

1. Heat the oil in a large sauté pan and fry the onion for 5 minutes. Add the garlic and cook for 2 more minutes then add the pork to the pan.

2. Stir-fry the pork for 2 minutes until it starts to colour, then stir in the mustards and the wine.

3. When the sauce starts to bubble, add the broccoli and stir to coat in the juices.

4. Pour in the double cream and bring to a gentle simmer, then put the lid on and cook for 4 minutes.

5. Stir the lemon juice into the sauce and season with salt and pepper just before serving.

Nettle soup

SERVES: 4 | PREP TIME: 5 MINUTES | COOKING TIME: 10 MINUTES

INGREDIENTS

2 tbsp olive oil

1 onion, finely chopped

2 cloves garlic, crushed

150 g / 5 ½ oz / 5 cups stinging nettles, chopped

1 litre / 1 pint 16 fl. oz / 4 cups vegetable stock

METHOD

1. Heat the oil in a saucepan and fry the onion for 5 minutes or until softened. Add the garlic and cook for 2 more minutes then stir in the nettles.

2. Pour in the vegetable stock and bring to the boil, then add salt and pepper to taste.

3. Ladle into four warm bowls and serve immediately.

Mussels with chilli and lemongrass

SERVES: 4 | PREP TIME: 2 MINUTES | COOKING TIME: 8 MINUTES

INGREDIENTS

2 tbsp vegetable oil

1 clove of garlic, skin on

1 red chilli, halved and thinly sliced

1 lemongrass stem, thinly sliced

1 tbsp Thai yellow curry paste

900 g / 2 lb / 4 ½ cups live mussels, cleaned

400 ml / 14 fl. oz / 1 ⅔ cups fish stock

1 tsp caster (superfine) sugar

1 lime, juiced

1 tbsp chives, chopped

METHOD

1. Heat the oil in a wok and fry the garlic, chilli, lemongrass and curry paste for 2 minutes.

2. Add the mussels, stock and sugar to the pan and put on the lid.

3. Cook for 5 minutes or until the mussels have steamed open.

4. Stir in the lime juice and chives and serve immediately.

Farfalle with spiced winter vegetables

SERVES: 4 | PREP TIME: 5 MINUTES | COOKING TIME: 12 MINUTES

INGREDIENTS

2 carrots, cut into chunks

½ cauliflower, broken into florets

½ head broccoli, broken into florets

400 g / 14 oz / 4 cups farfalle pasta

4 tbsp olive oil

4 cloves garlic, crushed

½ tsp ground cumin

½ tsp ground coriander

½ tsp chilli flakes

METHOD

1. Bring a very large saucepan of water to the boil with half a tablespoon of salt. Add the carrots and cook for 2 minutes then the cauliflower and broccoli and cook for a further 4 minutes. Drain in a colander.

2. Add the farfalle to the pan and cook according to the packet instructions or until al dente.

3. Meanwhile, heat the olive oil in a large sauté pan and cook the garlic and spices for 2 minutes.

4. Add the drained vegetables and toss to coat in the spiced oil. Add half a ladle of the pasta cooking water and simmer over a low heat.

5. Drain the pasta and stir it into the sauté pan then divide it between four bowls.

Chicken, noodle and shiitake stir-fry

SERVES: 4 | PREP TIME: 5 MINUTES | COOKING TIME: 15 MINUTES

INGREDIENTS

200 g / 7 oz / 2 cups Pho or Pad Thai rice noodles

3 tbsp vegetable oil

2 cloves of garlic, thinly sliced

1 tbsp root ginger, thinly sliced

2 shallots, sliced

100 g / 3 ½ oz / 1 cup shiitake mushrooms, thinly sliced

200 g / 7 oz / 1 ¼ cups chicken breast, thinly sliced

2 tbsp light soy sauce

chopped coriander (cilantro) to garnish

METHOD

1. Cook the noodles in boiling salted water according to the packet instructions or until al dente, then drain well.

2. Heat the oil in a large wok and fry the garlic, ginger, shallots and mushrooms for 2 minutes.

3. Add the chicken and stir-fry for 3 minutes or until just cooked through.

4. Add the soy sauce and noodles and stir-fry for 2 more minutes.

5. Serve immediately, garnished with coriander.

Tuna steaks with tomato and olive sauce

SERVES: 2 | PREP TIME: 10 MINUTES | COOKING TIME: 15-20 MINUTES

INGREDIENTS

200 g / 7 oz / 1 cup tomatoes

6 tbsp extra virgin olive oil

1 onion, quartered and sliced

1 tbsp red wine vinegar

50 g / 1 ¾ oz / ⅓ cup black olives, pitted

2 tuna steaks

a few sprigs of oregano

METHOD

1. Score a cross in the top of the tomatoes, then blanch them in boiling water for 30 seconds. When the skins start to curl, remove the tomatoes and dunk them in a bowl of cold water. Peel off and discard the skins, then finely chop the tomato flesh.

2. Meanwhile, heat 4 tablespoons of the oil in a frying pan and fry the onion for 5 minutes. Add a pinch of salt and the vinegar and bubble away almost to nothing. Add the tomatoes and olives and cook over a low heat.

3. Preheat a griddle pan. Brush the tuna steaks with the rest of the oil then griddle them for 8 minutes. Spoon the tomato sauce onto a serving plate and arrange the tuna steaks on top.

Chicken and mango stir-fry

SERVES: 4 | PREP TIME: 5 MINUTES | COOKING TIME: 8 MINUTES

INGREDIENTS

3 tbsp vegetable oil
2 cloves garlic, finely chopped
1 tbsp root ginger, finely chopped
1 red chilli, halved and sliced
200 g / 7 oz / 1 ¼ cups chicken breast, sliced
1 carrot, julienned
1 mango, peeled, stoned and cut into strips
2 tbsp rice wine or dry sherry
2 tbsp runny honey
1 tbsp light soy sauce

METHOD

1. Heat the oil in a large wok and fry the garlic, ginger and chilli for 30 seconds.

2. Add the chicken and carrot and stir-fry for 2 minutes then add the mango and stir-fry for another 2 minutes.

3. Mix the rice wine with the honey and soy and add it to the wok.

4. Stir-fry for 2 more minutes then serve immediately.

Cod with balsamic onions

SERVES: 2 | PREP TIME: 20 MINUTES | COOKING TIME: 18 MINUTES

INGREDIENTS

150 g / 5 ½ oz / ⅔ cup bulgur wheat

1 large onion, quartered and finely sliced

4 tbsp olive oil

2 tbsp balsamic vinegar

2 large cod steaks

METHOD

1. Put the bulgur wheat in a bowl and pour over enough boiling water to just cover it. Cover the bowl tightly and leave to soak for 15 minutes.

2. Fry the onion in half the oil for 10 minutes or until starting to caramelise then stir in the balsamic vinegar.

3. Arrange the cod steaks in a shallow bowl and pour the balsamic onion mixture over the top. Cover the bowl with clingfilm and transfer it to a steamer. Steam for 8 minutes.

4. Stir the rest of the oil into the bulgur wheat and season with salt and pepper. Split it between two warm plates and top with the cod and balsamic onions.

Chicken noodle curry

SERVES: 2 | PREP TIME: 10 MINUTES | COOKING TIME: 10 MINUTES

INGREDIENTS

2 skinless chicken breasts, sliced

2 tbsp Thai yellow curry paste

150 g / 5 ½ oz / 2 cups fine rice noodles

2 tbsp vegetable oil

200 ml / 7 fl. oz / ¾ cup coconut milk

2 tbsp coriander leaves, chopped

METHOD

1. Coat the chicken pieces with the curry paste and leave to marinate for 10 minutes.

2. Meanwhile, cover the noodles in boiling water and leave to soften for 5 minutes. Drain well.

3. Heat the oil in a wok and stir-fry the marinated chicken for 5 minutes or until cooked through.

4. Add the coconut milk and bring to a simmer, then add the noodles and cook for 2 minutes or until tender.

5. Garnish with coriander and serve.

Stir-fried vegetables

SERVES: 4 | PREP TIME: 2 MINUTES | COOKING TIME: 6 MINUTES

INGREDIENTS

2 tbsp vegetable oil

2 cloves garlic, finely chopped

1 tbsp root ginger, finely chopped

1 fennel bulb, thinly sliced

½ Chinese cabbage, shredded

1 courgette, diced

1 red pepper, julienned

2 tomatoes, cut into wedges

2 tbsp rice wine or dry sherry

1 tsp caster (superfine) sugar

1 tbsp light soy sauce

METHOD

1. Heat the oil in a large wok and fry the garlic and ginger for 30 seconds.

2. Add the vegetables and stir-fry for 4 minutes.

3. Mix the rice wine, sugar and soy together and add it to the wok.

4. Stir-fry for 1 more minute then serve immediately.

Ackee and saltfish

SERVES: 4 | PREP TIME: 5 MINUTES | COOKING TIME: 12 MINUTES

INGREDIENTS

3 tbsp olive oil

1 onion, sliced

1 red pepper, diced

1 red chilli, finely chopped

400 g / 14 oz / 2 cups salt cod, pre-soaked and cubed

400 g / 14 oz / 2 cups canned ackee, drained

1 tbsp fresh thyme leaves

1 lime, cut into wedges

METHOD

1. Heat the oil in a large sauté pan and fry the onion, peppers and chilli for 8 minutes or until softened.

2. Dry the salt cod on some kitchen paper and add it to the pan with the drained ackee.

3. Stir fry for 4 minutes or until cooked through then season with plenty of black pepper.

4. Divide between four warm plates and serve with the lime wedges to be squeezed over at the table.

Smoked chicken risotto

SERVES: 2 | PREP TIME: 5 MINUTES | COOKING TIME: 25 MINUTES

INGREDIENTS

1 litre / 1 pint 15 fl. oz / 4 cups good quality
chicken stock

2 tbsp olive oil

1 onion, finely chopped

2 cloves of garlic, crushed

150 g / 5 ½ oz / ¾ cup risotto rice

50 g / 1 ¾ oz / ½ cup Parmesan, finely grated

1 smoked chicken breast, sliced

METHOD

1. Heat the stock in a saucepan. Heat the
   olive oil in a sauté pan and gently fry
   the onion for 5 minutes. Add the garlic and
   cook for 2 more minutes then stir in the rice.
   When it is well coated with the oil,
   add 2 ladles of the hot stock.

2. Cook, stirring occasionally, until most of
   the stock has been absorbed before
   adding the next 2 ladles. Continue for
   15 minutes or until the rice is just tender.

3. Stir in the Parmesan and season with salt
   and pepper. Cover the pan and take off
   the heat to rest for 4 minutes. Spoon the
   risotto into warm bowls and lay the
   smoked chicken slices on top.

Chicken stir-fry with yogurt sauce

SERVES: 2 | PREP TIME: 5 MINUTES | COOKING TIME: 10 MINUTES

INGREDIENTS

2 tbsps olive oil

2 large boneless skinless chicken breasts

1 red pepper

1 red chilli (chili)

1 red onion

4 cherry tomatoes, halved

2 cloves garlic

FOR THE SAUCE:

100g natural plain yogurt

1 tablespoon lime juice

2 tsp Thai garlic chilli (chili) paste

1 clove garlic

TO SERVE:

nan bread

METHOD

1. Chop the chicken breasts into smaller pieces and sauté in heated olive oil. Chop the onions, tomatoes and peppers and add. Cook on a medium heat for about 8 minutes, or until browned. Add seasoning. Once browned, mince the garlic and add to the pan. Cook for a further 2 minutes.

2. Meanwhile, for the sauce, combine 1 cup yogurt, 2 teaspoons of the Thai chilli (chili) paste, one minced garlic clove, and 1 tablespoon lime juice and mix until combined.

3. Remove the stir-fry from the pan, and serve with a garnish of your choice on the nan bread, with the yogurt sauce as a side.

Chicken, tomato and nasturtium salad

SERVES: 4 | PREPARATION TIME: 5 MINUTES

INGREDIENTS

2 cooked chicken breasts, sliced

200 g / 7 oz / 2 cups cherry tomatoes, halved

200 g / 7 oz / 2 cups yellow cherry tomatoes, halved

4 spring onions (scallions), sliced lengthways

2 tbsp thyme leaves

4 tbsp extra virgin olive oil

a handful of nasturtium flowers

METHOD

1. Arrange the chicken, tomatoes and spring onions on four plates and sprinkle over the thyme.

2. Drizzle with olive oil and season with salt and pepper then garnish with the nasturtiums.

Tuna steaks with herb salsa

SERVES: 2 | PREP TIME: 5 MINUTES | COOKING TIME: 8 MINUTES

INGREDIENTS

2 tuna steaks

1 tbsp olive oil

FOR THE SALSA:

1 onion, peeled

a small bunch flat leaf parsley

1 tbsp mint leaves

1 tbsp capers

½ lemon, juiced

2 tbsp olive oil

METHOD

1. Preheat a griddle pan until smoking hot.

2. Brush the tuna steaks with the oil and season well with salt and pepper.

3. Griddle the steaks for 4 minutes then turn them over and cook for another 4 minutes or until done to your liking.

4. Meanwhile, chop the onion finely then add the herbs and capers to the board and chop them all together to create a coarse salsa.

5. Stir in the lemon juice and olive oil and season with salt and pepper.

6. Serve the tuna with a simple tomato and cucumber salad and the salsa spooned on top.

Spicy chicken salad

SERVES: 4 | PREP TIME: 5 MINUTES | COOKING TIME: 15-20 MINUTES

●●●●●●●●●●●●●●●●●●●●●●●●●

INGREDIENTS

½ lemon, juiced

2 tbsp sweet chilli (chili) sauce

1 tsp fennel seeds, finely ground

2 tbsp extra virgin olive oil, plus extra for drizzling

4 skinless chicken breasts, cut into large chunks

2 handfuls green mixed leaf salad

8 cherry tomatoes, halved

¼ cucumber, thinly sliced

1 handful basil leaves, washed

METHOD

1. Preheat the oven to 220°C (200°C fan) / 425F / gas 7.

2. Mix the lemon juice, chilli sauce, fennel seeds and oil in a bowl. Add the chicken chunks to the bowl and stir until coated.

3. Spread the coated chicken out on a non-stick baking tray and roast in the oven for 15-20 minutes or until browned on the outside and fully cooked.

4. While the chicken is cooking, divide the salad leaves, halved tomatoes and cucumber slices between four plates and pour over a drizzle of olive oil.

5. Once cooked, arrange the chicken on top of the salad and garnish each plate with a few basil leaves.

Pork chops with potatoes

SERVES: 2 | PREP TIME: 10 MINUTES | COOKING TIME: 20 MINUTES

INGREDIENTS

10 new potatoes, halved

2 woody sprigs of rosemary

2 pork chops

3 tbsp olive oil

salt and ground black pepper

2 tbsp thyme leaves

METHOD

1. Boil the potatoes in water for 12 minutes or until tender. Drain well. Meanwhile, preheat the grill to its highest setting.

2. Strip most of the leaves off the rosemary sprigs and thread the potatoes onto the woody stems.

3. Brush the pork and potatoes with half the oil and season with salt, black pepper and thyme.

4. Grill the cooked potato skewers for just 2 minutes, to crisp the skin.

5. Meanwhile, grill the chops for 4 minutes on each side, using the grilling plate to create char marks on the chops, if desired.

6. Divide the pork and potatoes between two warm plates (the potatoes can be served on the rosemary skewers or chopped into quarters).

Green quinoa salad

SERVES: 2 | PREP TIME: 5 MINUTES | COOKING TIME: 15 MINUTES

INGREDIENTS

½ head of broccoli, florets only

100 g / 3 ½ oz / ½ cup quinoa

1 lemon, juice

1 tsp olive oil

salt and freshly ground black pepper

1 avocado, peeled and diced

½ cucumber, cubed

a handful of basil leaves

METHOD

1. Boil the broccoli in a pan of boiling salted water for 4–5 minutes until softened. Drain and chop into smaller pieces.

2. Cook the quinoa as per the packed instructions, drain and spread over a baking tray to cool.

3. Mix the broccoli, quinoa, lemon juice and olive oil together and season with salt and black pepper to taste.

4. Mix the avocado and cucumber through the quinoa salad and divide between two serving plates.

5. Scatter of the basil leaves.

Tagliatelle with pesto

SERVES: 2 | PREP TIME: 5 MINUTES | COOKING TIME: 15 MINUTES

INGREDIENTS

200 g / 7 oz tagliatelle

a large bunch of basil, chopped

a large bunch of parsley, chopped

1 clove garlic

25 g / 1 oz / ¼ cup pine nuts

50 ml / 1 ¾ fl. oz / ¼ cup extra virgin olive oil

1 lemon, zest and juice

25 g / 1 oz / ¼ cup parmesan cheese, grated

METHOD

1. Place the pasta into a pan of salted boiling water and cook for 12–15 minutes until softened. Drain and return to the pan.

2. Place the remaining ingredients into a blender and blend for 1 minute until combined. If a little thick add some more oil. Season with salt and black pepper to taste.

3. Add a large spoonful of the pesto to the pasta, and mix to thoroughly coat the pasta with the pesto.

4. Spoon into warmed serving bowls and garnish with any additional basil leaves.

5. Any leftover pesto will keep in the refrigerator for 2–3 days.

Spaghetti and meatballs

SERVES: 2 | PREP TIME: 5 MINUTES | COOKING TIME: 15 MINUTES

INGREDIENTS

120 g / 4 ¼ oz spaghetti

300 g / 10 ½ oz Italian style sausages

1 tbsp breadcrumbs

50 g / 1 ¾ oz / ½ cup parmesan cheese, grated

1 tbsp olive oil

200 g / 7 oz tomato pasta sauce

a handful of basil leaves

1 red chilli (chili), sliced

METHOD

1. Place the spaghetti into a pan of salted boiling water and cook as per the packet instructions.

2. Cut open the sausages and combine with the breadcrumbs and parmesan cheese. Mix together with your hands until combined and form into balls roughly the size of a golf ball.

3. Heat the oil in a frying pan and add the meatballs. Brown on all sides.

4. Once the meatballs have been cooking for around 12 minutes add the sauce to the pan to warm through for 2–3 minutes. Mix through the pasta to coat in the sauce.

5. Divide between two warmed plates to serve and season with salt and black pepper and garnish with the basil leaves and sliced chilli.

Creamy carrot soup

SERVES: 2-4 | PREP TIME: 5 MINUTES | COOKING TIME: 20 MINUTES

INGREDIENTS

1 tbsp olive oil

600 g / 1 lbs 3 oz / 4 ¾ cups carrots, grated

1 onion, grated

2 celery sticks, sliced

1 clove of garlic, minced

1 ½ l / 50 fl. oz / 6 cups chicken or vegetable stock

50 ml / 1 ¾ fl. oz / ¼ cup double (heavy) cream

salt and freshly ground black pepper

flat-leaved parsley, to garnish

METHOD

1. Heat the oil in a large casserole pan or saucepan. Add the carrots, onions, celery and garlic and fry for 2–3 minutes until fragrant and softened.

2. Pour the stock into the pan and turn up the heat until boiling. Turn back down to a simmer and cover, leaving to cook for a further 12–15 minutes.

3. Using a hand blender, blend the soup until smooth. Pour in the cream and season with salt and black pepper to taste.

4. Pour into serving bowls and garnish with parsley, pepper and a drizzle of oil.

Chicken and vegetable broth

SERVES: 2 | PREP TIME: 5 MINUTES | COOKING TIME: 20 MINUTES

INGREDIENTS

50 g / 1 ¾ oz farfalle

1 tbsp vegetable oil

2 potatoes, peeled and cubed

2 carrots, peeled and diced

1 stick of celery, sliced

½ red pepper, finely sliced

750 ml / 25 ⅓ fl. oz / 3 cups vegetable stock

200 g / 7 oz leftover roast chicken, shredded

50 g / 1 ¾ oz / ⅓ cup peas, frozen

50 g / 1 ¾ oz / ⅓ cup sweetcorn, frozen

a handful of basil leaves

salt and freshly ground black pepper

METHOD

1. Place the pasta into a pan of salted boiling water and cook as per the packet instructions. Drain and set aside.

2. Heat the oil in a large casserole pan over a medium heat. Add the potatoes, carrots, celery and pepper. Fry for 4–5 minutes until softened.

3. Pour in the vegetable stock and turn up the heat until boiling. Once boiling turn back down to a simmer, add the roast chicken to the pan, cover and leave for 12-15 minutes adding the peas and sweetcorn after 5 minutes.

4. Add the basil leaves to the broth and season with salt and black pepper to taste. Check that the vegetables are cooked, if so add the pasta to the pan.

5. Serve in bowls with additional basil leaves as a garnish.

Chicken with apples and cider

SERVES: 2 | PREP TIME: 5 MINUTES | COOKING TIME: 20 MINUTES

INGREDIENTS

1 tbsp olive oil

400 g / 14 oz chicken breast, diced

1 shallot, chopped

1 clove of garlic, minced

1 apple, cored and chopped

250 ml / 8 ½ fl. oz / 1 cup apple cider

150 ml / 5 ¼ fl. oz / ⅔ cup double (heavy) cream

1 lemon, juiced

salt and freshly ground black pepper

2 spring onions (scallions), diced

METHOD

1. Heat the oil in a large non-stick pan over a medium high heat. Add the chicken and cook for 2–3 minutes until browned. Add the shallots and garlic to the pan and cook for a minute until fragrant and the shallots have softened.

2. Add the apple to the pan and pour in the cider. Leave to bubble and reduce for 3–4 minutes until the alcohol has cooked off.

3. Pour the cream into the pan and reduce the heat to a simmer. Leave to cook for 10–12 minutes until the chicken is cooked through.

4. Taste and add as much lemon juice as you feel is needed. Season with salt and black pepper to taste.

5. Add to serving plates and garnish with the spring onions.

Stuffed conchiglie

SERVES: 4 | PREP TIME: 5 MINUTES | COOKING TIME: 20 MINUTES

INGREDIENTS

400 g / 14 oz conchiglie

2 tbsp olive oil

300 g / 10 ½ oz beef mince

2 cloves of garlic, minced

1 tsp dried oregano

1 tsp dried basil

400 g / 14 oz canned chopped tomatoes

100 g / 3 ½ oz / 1 cup mozzarella cheese, grated

METHOD

1. Preheat the grill to high.

2. Cook the pasta as per the packet instructions, drain and set aside.

3. Heat the oil over a medium heat in a frying pan. Add the beef and brown and break up into smaller pieces. Add the garlic, herbs and tomatoes and season with salt and black pepper before covering and cooking for 15 minutes.

4. Spoon the cooked beef into the pasta shells and place into an ovenproof dish. Spoon over any remaining sauce and top with the grated cheese.

5. Place under the hot grill for 3–5 minutes until the cheese has melted and started to brown in places.

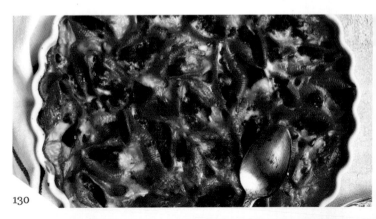

Tortiglione bolognese

SERVES: 2 | PREP TIME: 5 MINUTES | COOKING TIME: 15 MINUTES

••••••••••••••••••••••••••

INGREDIENTS

100 g / 3 ½ oz. tortiglione

1 tbsp olive oil

1 shallot, diced

1 clove of garlic, minced

300 g / 10 ½ oz. beef mince

1 tbsp tomato puree

125 ml / 4 ½ fl. oz / ½ cup red wine

50 g / 1 ¾ oz. cherry tomatoes, halved

50 g / 1 ¾ oz. / ⅓ cup black olives

A handful of basil leaves

50 g / 1 ¾ oz. / ½ cup parmesan cheese, grated

METHOD

1. Cook the pasta as per the packet instructions, drain retaining some of the water from the pan.

2. Heat the oil in a frying pan and add the shallot and garlic. Cook for 1–2 minutes.

3. Add the beef mince and brown the mean breaking it up into smaller pieces. Add the tomato puree and mix through the beef.

4. Pour the wine into the pan and turn the heat up for 3–4 minutes to cook off the alcohol. Turn the heat back down and add the tomatoes and olives to the pan. Cook for a further 10 minutes, and season the sauce to taste adding some of the reserved pasta water if it becomes too dry.

5. Mix the cooked pasta through the sauce and add to serving plates. Garnish with the basil leaves and top with the grated cheese.

Grilled chicken skewers

SERVES: 2 | PREP TIME: 5 MINUTES | COOKING TIME: 15 MINUTES

INGREDIENTS

2 tsp soy sauce

1 tsp sesame oil

1 lemon, juiced

1 tsp honey

1 tsp Chinese five spice

400 g / 14 oz. chicken breasts, diced

1 tbsp sesame seeds

METHOD

1. Preheat the grill or a griddle pan to a medium heat. Place some wooden skewers into water to soak.

2. Combine the soy, sesame oil, lemon juice, honey and five spice in a bowl.

3. Add the chicken to the marinade and mix to coat in the sauce.

4. Place the chicken onto the skewers before placing under the grill or onto the griddle pan.

5. Cook for 12–15 minutes turning occasionally to ensure they are evenly cooked on all sides.

6. Serve with rice, salad or on their own with a wedge of lemon.

Yellow split pea soup

SERVES: 4 | PREP TIME: 5 MINUTES | COOKING TIME: 20 MINUTES

INGREDIENTS

250 g / 9 oz. yellow split peas, soaked overnight

1 tbsp olive oil

1 onions, diced

1 clove of garlic, chopped

1 celery stick, sliced

200 g / 7 oz. bacon lardons

2 potatoes, peeled and diced

750 ml / 25 ⅓ fl. oz / 3 cups chicken or vegetable stock

METHOD

1. Drain the peas and rinse in cold water.

2. Heat the oil in a large pan with a lid. Add the onions and cook for 2–3 minutes until softened. Add the garlic and celery and fry for a further minute before adding the bacon and potatoes. Cook for a further couple of minutes until the bacon has started to colour at the edges.

3. Add the peas to the pan and pour over the stock. Turn up the heat until boiling before covering and turning down to a simmer. Cook for 12–15 minutes until the potatoes are cooked and the peas are tender.

4. Season with salt and black pepper to taste before serving.

Avocado salad with egg

SERVES: 1 | PREP TIME: 5 MINUTES | COOKING TIME: 15 MINUTES

INGREDIENTS

50 g / 1 ¾ oz / ¼ cup easy cook long grain rice

½ head broccoli, florets only

1 avocado, peeled and chopped

1 lemon, juiced

1 tsp oil

1 egg

METHOD

1. Cook the rice as per the packet instructions, drain and set aside.

2. Place the broccoli into a pan of salted boiling water, cook for 6–8 minutes and drain.

3. Combine the cooked rice, broccoli and the avocado. Add the lemon juice and season with salt and black pepper.

4. Heat the oil in a non-stick frying pan and break the egg into the pan. Fry for 2–3 minutes until the bottom is starting to crisp and the white has cooked.

5. Place the rice and avocado salad onto a serving plate and top with the fried egg.

Nachos

SERVES: 2-4 | PREPARATION TIME: 10 MINUTES

••••••••••••••••••••••••

INGREDIENTS

2 avocados, peeled and chopped

1 lime, juiced

1 tsp chilli (chili) flakes (optional)

200 g / 7 oz tortilla chips

1 red onion, finely chopped

100 g / 3 ½ oz cherry tomatoes, finely chopped

100 g / 3 ½ oz / 1 cup cheddar cheese, grated

50 g / 1 ¾ oz sliced green jalapenos

a small bunch of coriander (cilantro).

METHOD

1. Place the avocado into a bowl and mash with the lime juice and chilli flakes to make a guacamole.

2. Place a layer of the tortilla chips into a serving bowl. Top with some of the onion, tomato and cheese.

3. Repeat the above step a couple of times until all the ingredients have been used.

4. Top the dish with the guacamole, sliced jalapenos and coriander.

Pork tacos

SERVES: 2-4 | PREP TIME: 5 MINUTES | COOKING TIME: 15 MINUTES

INGREDIENTS

4 small tortilla wraps

350 g / 12 ¼ oz. pork, diced

1 tsp ground cumin

1 tsp ground coriander (cilantro)

1 tsp paprika

1 tsp chilli (chili) powder

1 tbsp olive oil

1 onion, sliced

1 red pepper, sliced

1 courgette (zucchini), sliced

1 lemon, juiced

METHOD

1. Preheat the oven to 200°C (180°C fan) / 400F / gas 6.

2. Turn a muffin tin upside down and place the tortilla wraps into the grooves to form a taco shape. Bake in the oven for 12–15 minutes until crisp and retain the curved shape.

3. Combine the pork and spices in a mixing bowl and season with salt and black pepper.

4. Heat oil in a frying pan over a medium high heat. Add the pork and fry for 2–3 minutes until browned. Add the vegetables to the pan and stir fry for a further 8–10 minutes until the pork and vegetables are cooked. Season to taste and mix through the lemon juice.

5. Spoon the pork and vegetables into the prepared taco shells and serve.

Pork, honey and sesame stir-fry

SERVES: 2 | PREP TIME: 4 MINUTES | COOKING TIME: 8 MINUTES

INGREDIENTS

3 tbsp vegetable oil

1 onion, thinly sliced

2 cloves of garlic, finely chopped

225 g / 8 oz / 1 ½ cups pork steak, sliced

2 tbsp sesame seeds

1 red pepper, julienned

2 tbsp rice wine or dry sherry

2 tbsp runny honey

1 tbsp dark soy sauce

METHOD

1. Heat the oil in a large wok and fry the onion for 2 minutes.

2. Add the garlic, pork and sesame seeds and stir-fry for 2 more minutes then add the peppers.

3. Stir-fry for 2 minutes then mix the rice wine with the honey and soy and add it to the wok.

4. Stir-fry until it reduced to a sticky glaze then serve immediately.

Beetroot burger with cucumber salad

SERVES: 2 | PREP TIME: 10 MINUTES | COOKING TIME: 10 MINUTES

INGREDIENTS

200 g / 7 oz raw beetroot, grated

2 spring onions (scallions), sliced

1 lemon, zest and juice

100 g / 3 ½ oz feta, crumbled

1 tbsp flour

1 egg beaten

2 tbsp olive oil

1 cucumber, cut into ribbons

a handful of flat-leaved parsley, chopped

METHOD

1. Place the beetroot into a cloth and squeeze out as much moisture as possible.

2. Combine the beetroot, spring onions, lemon zest and half the juice, feta, flour and egg in a mixing bowl and combine. Use your hands to form into burger shapes.

3. Heat half the oil in a non-stick pan over a medium heat. Fry the burger for 3–4 minutes on each side.

4. Mix the cucumbers ribbons, remaining lemon juice and oil in a bowl. Add the parsley and mix through before seasoning with salt and black pepper.

5. Serve the burgers with the cucumber salad.

Chicken and avocado wraps

SERVES: 1-2 | PREP TIME: 5 MINUTES | COOKING TIME: 15 MINUTES

INGREDIENTS

1 tbsp olive oil

250 g / 9 oz chicken breast, thinly sliced

1 tsp paprika

1 tsp cayenne

1 avocado, peeled and sliced

1 lemon, juiced

a small bunch of coriander (cilantro), chopped

2 tortilla wraps

2 tbsp mayonnaise

METHOD

1. Heat the oil in a pan and add the chicken. Brown for a couple of minutes before adding the paprika and cayenne. Toss the chicken in the spices before adding a splash of water. Continue to cook for 8–10 minutes until the chicken is cooked.

2. Mix the chicken with the avocado and squeeze over the lemon juice. Season with salt and black pepper before stirring through the coriander.

3. Place the wraps onto a serving plate and add a spoonful of mayonnaise in the centre. Spoon the chicken and avocado mixture on top of the mayonnaise.

4. Fold the wrap over the top and bottom edges of the filling before rolling the wrap from one of the longer edges, folding the wrap under the filling.

5. Serve immediately or great for a lunch box or picnic if wrapped in foil to hold the shape.

Salmon steak salad

SERVES: 4 | PREP TIME: 10-15 MINUTES | COOKING TIME: 15 MINUTES

INGREDIENTS

4 x 150 g / 5 oz salmon steaks

2 tbsp olive oil

2 handfuls mixed green leaf salad

1 pinch of micro herbs

1 tbsp flaked almonds (slivers)

METHOD

1. Preheat the oven to 220°C (200°C fan) / 425F / gas 7.

2. Sit the salmon on a baking tray and drizzle with olive oil and season liberally with salt and pepper.

3. Roast for 10 minutes or until firm to the touch.

4. Meanwhile, arrange the mixed salad leaves on the plate.

5. Once the salmon is cooked, place it on top of the bed of salad leaves and sprinkle with the micro herbs and flaked almonds on top before serving.

Vegetable bowl with chicken

SERVES: 1 | PREPARATION TIME: 5 MINUTES

INGREDIENTS

50 g / 1 ¾ oz lamb's lettuce

50 g / 1 ¾ oz cherry tomatoes

1 avocado

½ red onion

¼ cucumber

50 g / 1 ¾ oz chickpeas (garbanzo beans)

1 chicken breast, cooked

1 lemon wedge

salt and freshly ground black pepper

1 tbsp extra virgin olive oil

METHOD

1. Wash the salad leave and prepare the salad ingredients by peeling, chopping and slicing as required.

2. The chickpeas should be drained from the can and rinsed.

3. Slice the chicken breast into bite sized pieces.

4. Arrange the ingredients in a serving bowl with the lemon wedge before seasoning with salt and black pepper and drizzling over the oil.

Tagliatelle with broccoli and parmesan

SERVES: 2 | PREP TIME: 2 MINUTES | COOKING TIME: 12 MINUTES

INGREDIENTS

200 g / 7 oz / 2 cups tagliatelle

200 g / 7 oz / 2 cups broccoli, broken into small florets

4 tbsp olive oil

3 cloves garlic, crushed

75 g / 2 ½ oz / ¾ cup Parmesan, finely grated

METHOD

1. Cook the tagliatelle in boiling salted water according to the packet instructions or until al dente.

2. Meanwhile, blanch the broccoli in boiling salted water for 3–4 minutes or until just tender. Drain well.

3. Heat the oil in a sauté pan and fry the garlic for 2 minutes. Add the drained broccoli and cook, stirring occasionally, for 3 minutes so it can take on the flavour from the oil. Season to taste with salt and pepper.

4. Reserve a couple of ladles of pasta water and drain the rest.

5. Stir the pasta into the broccoli pan with 3 tablespoons of the pasta water and shake to emulsify with the oil. If it looks a bit dry, add some more pasta water.

6. Divide between two warm bowls and top with plenty of Parmesan.

Cook's Corner

Quick and Easy

Desserts

Donut balls

MAKES: 8 | PREP TIME: 10 MINUTES | COOKING TIME: 10 MINUTES

INGREDIENTS

125 g / 4 ¼ oz / ¾ cup plain (all-purpose) flour

1 tsp baking powder

1 tsp bicarbonate of (baking) soda

1 large free-range egg

170 g / 2 ½ oz / ⅓ cup caster (superfine) sugar

50 ml / 1 ¾ fl. oz / ¼ cup milk

50 g / 1 ¾ oz / ¼ cup buttermilk

30 g unsalted butter, melted

1 tsp vanilla extract

1 tsp cinnamon

2 tbsp chocolate sauce

METHOD

1. Preheat a deep fat fryer 180°C (160°C fan) / 350F / gas 4. Combine the flour, baking powder and bicarbonate of soda in a large mixing bowl.

2. In a separate bowl, whisk together the egg, half the sugar, milk, buttermilk, butter and vanilla extract. Pour the wet ingredients into the dry and mix to combine. The batter needs to be fairly thick, take care not to over mix.

3. Carefully spoon the mixture into the hot oil, shaping roughly into a ball shape.

4. Fry for 2–3 minutes in the oil until golden, turning as necessary.

5. Drain onto kitchen paper before rolling in a mixture of the remaining sugar and cinnamon.

6. Place into a serving bowl and spoon over the chocolate sauce.

Apple and cherry tartlets

MAKES: 8-10 | PREP TIME: 5 MINUTES | COOKING TIME: 15 MINUTES

INGREDIENTS

200 g / 7 oz sweet short crust pastry sheet

6 pink lady apples

25 g / 1 oz butter

2 tbsp soft brown sugar

1 tsp cinnamon

fresh cherries, to garnish

METHOD

1. Preheat the oven to 200°C (180°C fan) / 400F / gas 6. Lightly grease a muffin tin.

2. Roll out the pastry to 2mm thickness and cut out pastry cases using a round cutter.

3. Place into the muffin tin and prick the bases with a fork. Line with greaseproof paper and weigh down with baking beans. Blind bake in the oven for 10-12 minutes until golden, removing the greaseproof paper after 5 minutes. Remove to cool.

4. Peel and core the apples and chop into chunks.

5. Melt the butter and sugar together before adding the apples and cinnamon. Cook for 12–15 minutes until the apples start to break down. Blend to a smooth puree. Spoon the apple puree into the pastry cases and garnish with the cherries.

153

Coconut fool

SERVES: 4 | PREP TIME: 10 MINUTES | COOKING TIME: 2 MINUTES

INGREDIENTS

75 g / 2 ½ oz / ¾ cup desiccated coconut
300 ml / 10 ½ fl. oz / 1 ¼ cups double cream
300 g / 10 ½ oz / 1 ¼ cups coconut flavoured yogurt

METHOD

1. Preheat the grill to its highest setting.

2. Spread the coconut out on a baking sheet and toast under the hot grill until golden brown. Leave to cool.

3. Whip the cream until thick but not stiff, then fold in the yogurt and half of the toasted coconut.

4. Spoon the cream into four fool glasses and sprinkle over the remaining coconut.

Raspberry Eton mess

SERVES: 4 | PREPARATION TIME: 10 MINUTES

INGREDIENTS

300 g / 10 ½ oz / 2 ¼ cups raspberries

600 ml / 1 pint / 2 ½ cups double cream

4 meringue nests, crushed

METHOD

1. Press half the raspberries through a sieve to make a smooth sauce and discard the pips.

2. Whip the cream until it forms soft peaks then fold in the meringue pieces and all but 4 of the whole raspberries.

3. Swirl through the raspberry sauce and divide it between four sundae glasses then top each one with a raspberry.

Chocolate pancakes with mascarpone

SERVES: 2 | PREP TIME: 5 MINUTES | COOKING TIME: 15 MINUTES

INGREDIENTS

250 g / 9 oz / 1 ⅔ cups plain (all purpose) flour
50 g / 1 ¾ oz / ⅓ cup cocoa
1 egg
50 g / 1 ¾ oz. / ½ cup caster (superfine) sugar
1 tsp baking powder
150 ml / 5 ¼ fl. oz / ⅔ cup milk
1 tsp oil
300 g / 10 ½ oz mascarpone
50 g / 1 ¾ oz / ½ cup icing (confectioner's) sugar
1 tsp vanilla essence
100 g / 3 ½ oz chocolate sauce

METHOD

1. Combine the flour, cocoa, egg, sugar and baking powder in a mixing bowl. Mix together before adding the milk and whisking to a smooth batter without any lumps. Add a splash more milk if too thick, it should be roughly the consistency of double cream.

2. Heat the oil in a non-stick frying pan and once hot ladle some of the batter into the pan. Cook for 2–3 minutes until bubbles start to appear before flipping over and cook for a further minute on the other side. Repeat until all the batter has been used.

3. Whisk together the mascarpone, icing sugar and vanilla essence until it has thickened slightly.

4. To serve, layer the pancakes with the mascarpone in between each layer. Top with the chocolate sauce and garnish with fresh berries as desired.

Chocolate mousse

SERVES: 2 | PREP TIME: 15 MINUTES | COOKING TIME: 5 MINUTES

INGREDIENTS

100 g / 3 ½ oz. dark chocolate

568 ml / 19 ¼ fl. oz / 2 ⅓ cups double (heavy) cream

2 egg whites

50 g / 1 ¾ oz / ¼ cup caster (superfine) sugar

2 tbsp chocolate chips

METHOD

1. Break up the chocolate and place into a heatproof bowl.

2. Separate off a quarter of the cream and whisk until whipped. Heat the remaining cream in a pan until just simmering. Pour the warm cream over the chocolate whilst mixing until combined, set aside to cool.

3. Fold a spoonful of the chocolate mixture into the whipped cream and set aside.

4. Whisk the egg whites until soft peaks form. Gradually add the sugar whilst continuing to whisk until smooth and silky.

5. Fold the whisked egg whites through the chocolate mixture and spoon into serving glasses.

6. Place the chocolate whipped cream into a piping bag and pipe on top of the mousse.

7. Sprinkle over the chocolate chips.

Fruity jelly

SERVES: 4 | PREPARATION TIME: 15 MINUTES PLUS CHILLING

INGREDIENTS

125 g / 4 ½ oz / 1 cup strawberry jelly cubes

600 ml / 1 pint 2 fl. oz / 2 ⅔ cups boiling water

250 g / 9 oz / 2 cups raspberries, washed

250 g / 9 oz / 2 cups blackberries, washed

METHOD

1. Place the jelly cubes in a heatproof jug and pour over a third of the boiling water. Stir until the cubes have dissolved.

2. Top up the jug with the rest of the water and leave to cool for a few minutes.

3. Fill four heatproof dessert pots with a handful of blackberries and a handful of raspberries and then pour over the jelly liquid.

4. Place the filled dessert pots in the fridge until set.

5. These desserts will keep in the fridge for 2–3 days.

Summer berry chia dessert

SERVES: 2 | PREP TIME: 5 MINUTES | COOKING TIME: 15 MINUTES

INGREDIENTS

100 g / 3 ½ oz strawberry jam (jelly)

30 g chia seeds

300 g / 10 ½ oz natural yogurt

a handful of fresh blueberries

a handful of fresh strawberries, sliced in half

METHOD

1. Spoon the strawberry jam into the bottom of some serving bowls.

2. Mix the chia seeds and yogurt together. You could sweeten with honey if desired but the jam should add enough sweetness.

3. Spoon the yogurt mix over the jam and place into the fridge to chill for 12–15 minutes.

4. When ready to serve top with the berries.

Lemon tart

SERVES: 8 | PREP TIME: 5 MINUTES | COOKING TIME: 25 MINUTES

INGREDIENTS

3 lemons, juiced

175 g / 6 oz / ¾ cup caster (superfine) sugar

2 tsp cornflour

4 large eggs, beaten

225 ml / 8 fl. oz / ¾ cup double cream

1 pastry case

lemon zest to garnish

METHOD

1. Preheat the oven to 170°C (150° fan) / 340F / gas 3.

2. Stir the lemon juice into the caster sugar and cornflour to dissolve, then whisk in the eggs and cream.

3. Strain the mixture into the pastry case and bake for 25 minutes or until just set in the centre.

4. Garnish with lemon zest and serve warm or at room temperature.

Banana split

SERVES: 2 | PREPARATION TIME: 10 MINUTES

INGREDIENTS

150 ml / 5 ½ fl. oz / ¾ cup double cream

2 scoops of chocolate ice cream

2 scoops of vanilla ice cream

2 scoops of strawberry ice cream

2 bananas, peeled and halved lengthways

1 tbsp hazelnuts (cobnuts), chopped

strawberry ice cream sauce

METHOD

1. Whip the cream until thick then spoon it into a piping bag fitted with a large star nozzle.

2. Scoop the ice cream into two banana split bowls and pipe a swirl of cream at either end.

3. Tuck the banana halves down the sides and sprinkle with hazelnuts then drizzle over some strawberry sauce.

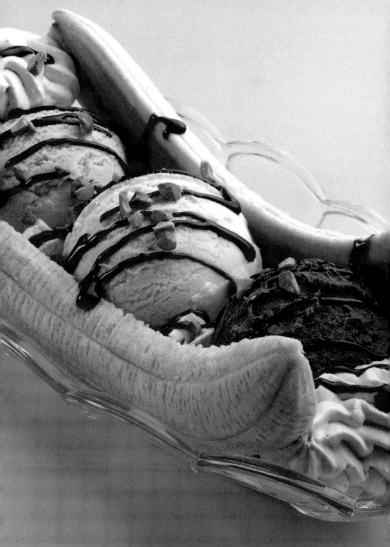

Chocolate fondue

SERVES: 4 | PREP TIME: 2 MINUTES | COOKING TIME: 4 MINUTES

INGREDIENTS

100 g / 3 ½ oz / ¾ cup milk chocolate

150 ml / 3 ½ fl. oz / ⅔ cup double cream

2 tbsp brandy

3 clementines, peeled

200 g / 7 oz / 1 cup strawberries, hulled and halved

METHOD

1. Chop the chocolate and put it in a fondue bowl.

2. Bring the cream and brandy to simmering point then pour it over the chocolate and stir until smooth.

3. Serve with the clementine segments and strawberries for dipping.

Banoffee dessert

SERVES: 4 | PREP TIME: 10 MINUTES | COOKING TIME: 10 MINUTES

INGREDIENTS

50 g / 1 ¾ oz / ¼ cup butter

50 g / 1 ¾ oz / ¼ cup dark brown sugar

200 g / 7 oz condensed milk

200 ml / 7 fl. oz / ¾ cup double (heavy) cream

4 bananas, sliced

100 g / 3 ½ oz shortbread thins

METHOD

1. Heat the butter and sugar in a pan until the sugar has melted. Add the condensed milk and stir through. Heat until boil and then turn off the heat and leave to cool.

2. Once cool divide the caramel between four serving dishes or glasses.

3. Whip the double cream until stiff.

4. Spoon the cream, sliced bananas and shortbread biscuits into the serving glasses on top of the caramel.

5. Serve immediately or place into the refrigerator until needed.

Amaretti fool

SERVES: 4 | PREPARATION TIME: 10 MINUTES

INGREDIENTS

50 g / 1 ¾ oz / ¼ cup butter

50 g / 1 ¾ oz / ¼ cup dark brown sugar

200 g / 7 oz condensed milk

200 ml / 7 fl. oz / ¾ cup double (heavy) cream

4 bananas, sliced

100 g / 3 ½ oz shortbread thins

METHOD

1. Heat the butter and sugar in a pan until the sugar has melted. Add the condensed milk and stir through. Heat until boil and then turn off the heat and leave to cool.

2. Once cool divide the caramel between four serving dishes or glasses.

3. Whip the double cream until stiff.

4. Spoon the cream, sliced bananas and shortbread biscuits into the serving glasses on top of the caramel.

5. Serve immediately or place into the refrigerator until needed.

Summer fruit compote with meringue

MAKES: 6 | PREP TIME: 20 MINUTES | COOKING TIME: 15 MINUTES

INGREDIENTS

450 g / 1 lb / 2 cups frozen summer fruits, defrosted

2 tbsp caster (superfine) sugar

1 vanilla pod, halved lengthways

FOR THE MERINGUE:

4 large egg whites

110 g / 4 oz / ½ cup caster (superfine) sugar

METHOD

1. Preheat the oven to 200°C (180° fan) / 390F / gas 6.

2. Put the fruit in a saucepan with the sugar and vanilla and cover with a lid.

3. Cook it over a medium heat for 5 minutes, stirring occasionally then discard the vanilla pod and spoon the compote into six oven-proof glasses or bowls.

4. Whisk the egg whites until stiff, then gradually add the sugar and whisk for several minutes until the mixture is thick and shiny.

5. Spoon the meringue into a piping bag, fitted with a large star nozzle, and pipe a big swirl of meringue on top of each compote.

6. Bake for 10 minutes or until the tops are golden brown.

Marmalade baguette and butter puddings

SERVES: 6 | PREP TIME: 10 MINUTES | COOKING TIME: 15-20 MINUTES

INGREDIENTS

1 baguette, thinly sliced

3 tbsp butter, softened

250 ml / 9 fl. oz / 1 cup whole milk

200 ml / 7 oz / ¾ cup double cream

4 large egg yolks

75 g / 2 ½ oz / ⅓ cup caster (superfine) sugar

4 tbsp marmalade

METHOD

1. Preheat the oven to 180°C (160° fan) / 355F / gas 4.

2. Spread the baguette with butter and arrange the slices in six small baking dishes.

3. Whisk the milk, cream, eggs and sugar together and pour it over the top, then press down on the baguette to help it soak up the liquid.

4. Melt the marmalade in a small saucepan then spoon it over the puddings.

5. Bake for 15–20 minutes or until the tops are golden brown.

Coffee chocolate mousse

SERVES: 2 | PREP TIME: 15 MINUTES | COOKING TIME: 5 MINUTES

INGREDIENTS

100 g / 3 ½ oz. chocolate

1 tsp espresso powder

500 ml / 17 fl. oz / 2 cups double (heavy) cream

50 g / 1 ¾ oz. chocolate cookies, broken

METHOD

1. Break the chocolate into a heatproof bowl suspended over some boiling water, taking care that the bowl is not touching the water.

2. Once the chocolate has melted remove from the heat and stir through the espresso powder.

3. Separate the cream into two bowls. Gently whip one of the bowls of cream until thickened but not whipped. Fold the melted chocolate and coffee through this cream.

4. Whip the second bowl of cream until whipped and stiffened.

5. Place alternate layers of coffee mousse and whipped cream into serving glasses placing a layer of broken cookies into the middle.

Coffee ice cream sundae

SERVES: 2 | PREPARATION TIME: 10 MINUTES

INGREDIENTS

150 ml / 5 ½ fl. oz / ⅔ cup double cream

2 shots fresh espresso

2 scoops of vanilla ice cream

2 scoops of coffee ice cream

4 Mikado biscuits

chocolate sprinkles and cocoa powder to garnish

METHOD

1. Whip the cream until thick then spoon it into a piping bag fitted with a large star nozzle.

2. Put an espresso shot in the bottom of two glass mugs and top with a scoop of vanilla ice cream.

3. Scoop in some coffee ice cream then pipe a swirl of cream on top of each one.

4. Garnish the sundaes with 2 chocolate-coated biscuits, chocolate sprinkles and a dusting of cocoa powder.

White chocolate fondue

SERVES: 4 | PREP TIME: 5 MINUTES | COOKING TIME: 4 MINUTES

INGREDIENTS

100 g / 3 ½ oz / ⅔ cup white chocolate
150 ml / 3 ½ fl. oz / ⅔ cup double cream
2 tbsp Cointreau
raspberries and brownie squares for dipping

METHOD

1. Chop the chocolate and put it in a fondue bowl.

2. Bring the cream and Cointreau to simmering point then pour it over the chocolate and stir until smooth.

3. Serve with the raspberries and brownie squares for dipping.

Banana, caramel and ice cream dessert

SERVES: 2-4 | PREP TIME: 10 MINUTES | COOKING TIME: 5 MINUTES

INGREDIENTS

1 tbsp butter

1 tbsp soft brown sugar

1 tbsp golden syrup

2 tbsp condensed milk

50 ml / 1 ¾ fl. oz / ¼ cup double (heavy) cream

2 bananas, sliced

500 ml / 17 fl. oz / 2 cups vanilla ice cream

25 g chopped almonds

METHOD

1. Heat the butter, sugar, golden syrup and condensed milk in a saucepan until the sugar has dissolved and when mixed the mixture forms a thick caramel.

2. Remove from the heat and stir through the cream, leave to cool while you prepare the rest of the dessert.

3. Combine the bananas and ice cream in serving bowls, spoon over the caramel sauce.

4. Serve with the chopped almonds sprinkled over the top.

Spiced pear and pineapple kebabs

SERVES: 4 | PREP TIME: 20 MINUTES | COOKING TIME: 6 MINUTES

INGREDIENTS

4 tbsp runny honey

1 star anise, plus extra to garnish

4 cloves

2 pears, quartered, cored and sliced

½ pineapple, peeled, cored and cut into large chunks

a few sprigs of mint

METHOD

1. Soak 8 wooden skewers in cold water for 20 minutes. Meanwhile, put the honey in a small saucepan with the spices and heat gently. Leave to infuse for 15 minutes.

2. Preheat the grill to its highest setting.

3. Thread alternate chunks of pear and pineapple onto the skewers and brush with the spiced honey. Grill the kebabs for 3 minutes on each side.

4. Transfer the kebabs to four warm plates and garnish with star anise and mint sprigs.

Cherry fool

SERVES: 4 | PREPARATION TIME: 10 MINUTES

INGREDIENTS

150 g / 5 ½ oz / ¾ cup cherries, stoned

2 tbsp kirsch

50 g / 1 ¾ oz / ½ cup icing (confectioner's) sugar

600 ml / 1 pint / 2 ½ cups double cream

METHOD

1. Put the cherries, kirsch and icing sugar in a food processor and pulse until finely chopped.

2. Whip the cream until thick then fold through the cherry mixture.

3. Spoon the mixture into four fool glasses and serve.

Lemon meringue pie

SERVES: 8 | PREP TIME: 15 MINUTES | COOKING TIME: 10 MINUTES

INGREDIENTS

1 pastry case

1 jar lemon curd

4 large egg whites

110 g / 4 oz / ½ cup caster (superfine) sugar

METHOD

1. Preheat the oven to 200°C (180° fan) / 390F / gas 6.

2. Fill the pastry case with lemon curd and smooth the top with a palette knife.

3. Whisk the egg whites until stiff, then gradually add the sugar and whisk until the mixture is thick and shiny.

4. Spoon the meringue on top of the lemon curd, making peaks with the spoon.

5. Bake for 10 minutes or until golden brown.

186

Caramelized spiced mangoes

SERVES: 2 | PREP TIME: 5 MINUTES | COOKING TIME: 15 MINUTES

INGREDIENTS

2 mangoes, peeled, stoned and cut into wedges

3 tbsp runny honey

2 tbsp dark rum

1 tbsp butter, melted

2 star anise

METHOD

1. Preheat the oven to 180°C (160° fan) / 355F / gas 4.

2. Arrange the mango wedges in a small baking dish.

3. Mix the honey with the rum, melted butter and star anise and pour it over the top.

4. Bake in the oven for 15 minutes or until the mango is soft and starting to caramelise at the edges.

Indulgent chocolate milkshake

SERVES: 2 | PREPARATION TIME: 10 MINUTES

●●●●●●●●●●●●●●●●●●●●●●●●

INGREDIENTS

6 tbsp dark chocolate chips

4 tbsp milk chocolate chips

1 tsp cinnamon powder

1 tsp cocoa powder

1 tsp white granulated sugar

500 ml / 17 fl. oz / 2 cups semi-skimmed milk

chocolate sauce, to drizzle

2 handfuls marshmallows

double (heavy) cream, whipped

METHOD

1. Blitz the dark chocolate chips, milk chocolate chips, cinnamon, cocoa powder, sugar and semi-skimmed milk in the blender, according to the manufacturer's instructions, until fully combined.

2. Meanwhile, drizzle some chocolate sauce on the insides of two tall glasses to make a decorative zigzag pattern. Once blended, divide the milkshake between both glasses, gently pouring it into the centre of each glass so that the chocolate sauce pattern is not washed away.

3. Then, top each milkshake with a handful of marshmallows and a generous helping of whipped cream.

Pear and pecan ice cream sundae

SERVES: 2 | PREP TIME: 5 MINUTES

INGREDIENTS

75 ml / 2 ½ fl. oz / 1/3 cup chocolate sauce
6 scoops good quality vanilla ice cream
6 canned pear halves in juice, drained
50 g / 1 ¾ oz / ½ cup pecan nuts, chopped
150 ml / 5 ½ fl. oz / 2/3 cup whipped cream
2 maraschino cherries

METHOD

1. Drizzle a little chocolate sauce into the bottom of two sundae glasses.

2. Layer up the ice cream scoops with the pears and pecan nuts, saving a few pecans for the garnish. Drizzle with chocolate sauce.

3. Spoon the whipped cream on top of the sundaes and garnish each one with a maraschino cherry and an extra sprinkle of pecans.

Cook's Corner

Quick and Easy

Snacks and sides

Potatoes with mushrooms

SERVES: 4 | PREP TIME: 5 MINUTES | COOKING TIME: 18 MINUTES

INGREDIENTS

800 g / 1 lb 12 oz / 5 ⅓ cup potatoes, cut in half

4 tbsp olive oil

½ small jar sun-dried tomato paste

50 g / 1 ¾ oz / ⅓ cup button mushrooms, chopped

50 g / 1 ¾ oz / ⅓ cup Cheddar cheese, finely grated

1 handful fresh parsley sprigs

METHOD

1. Boil the potatoes in salted water for 12 minutes then drain well and leave to steam dry for 2 minutes.

2. Heat the oil in a large frying pan then colour the potatoes for 3 minutes.

3. Transfer the potatoes to a grease-proof lined baking tray and top them with the tomato paste, chopped mushrooms, grated cheese and sprigs of parsley.

4. Put the potatoes under the grill for 2 minutes or until the cheese has melted.

5. Transfer the potatoes to four plates and serve immediately.

Sautéed new potatoes with oregano

SERVES: 4 | PREP TIME: 2 MINUTES | COOKING TIME: 20 MINUTES

INGREDIENTS

Sautéed New Potatoes with Oregano

800 g / 1 lb 12 oz / 5 ⅓ cup baby new potatoes

4 tbsp olive oil

2 tbsp fresh oregano leaves

METHOD

1. Boil the potatoes in salted water for 8 minutes then drain well and leave to steam dry for 2 minutes.

2. Heat the oil in a large sauté pan then fry the potatoes for 10 minutes or until golden on all sides.

3. Add the oregano to the pan with a big scrunch of sea salt flakes and stir well before serving.

Potato wedges

SERVES: 2-4 | PREP TIME: 5 MINUTES | COOKING TIME: 20 MINUTES

INGREDIENTS

400 g / 14 oz. Maris Piper potatoes

2 tbsp vegetable oil

Sea salt flakes

METHOD

1. Peel the potatoes and cut into wedges.

2. Place into a pan of salted boiling water and par boil for 5 minutes before draining. Sprinkle the drained potatoes with a generous amount of salt.

3. Heat the oil in a large frying pan over a medium high heat. Once hot carefully place the wedges into the oil. Fry in the oil without moving the wedges, turn them every 4–5 minutes or once they have turned golden.

4. Once golden on all sides and cooked through remove from the pan with a spatula or slotted spoon and place onto kitchen paper to soak up any excess oil.

5. Serve as a side or on their own with a dip.

Fresh broad bean salad

SERVES: 4 | PREP TIME: 10 MINUTES | COOKING TIME: 5 MINUTES

INGREDIENTS

2 shallots, finely chopped

3 tbsp sherry vinegar

2 tsp caster (superfine) sugar

600 g / 1 lb 5 oz / 5 ½ cups fresh broad beans, podded weight

4 tbsp extra virgin olive oil

a small bunch of chervil, chopped

METHOD

1. Put the shallots in a bowl with the vinegar, sugar and a big pinch of salt and leave to macerate for 10 minutes.

2. Meanwhile, blanch the broad beans in boiling water for 5 minutes then drain and refresh in cold water. Drain well.

3. Whisk the olive oil into the shallot vinegar and taste for seasoning then stir in the chervil and broad beans.

Prawn, coconut and lime leaf skewers

SERVES: 2 | PREP TIME: 5 MINUTES | COOKING TIME: 4 MINUTES

INGREDIENTS

20 raw king prawns, peeled
8 frozen lime leaves, defrosted
1 tbsp vegetable oil
30 g creamed coconut block, grated

METHOD

1. Preheat a griddle pan until smoking hot.

2. Thread the prawns and lime leaves onto 8 metal skewers.

3. Stir the oil into the creamed coconut and brush it over the prawns then griddle the skewers for 2 minutes on each side or until the prawns turn opaque.

Tuna and couscous salad

SERVES: 4 | PREP TIME: 5 MINUTES | COOKING TIME: 5 MINUTES

INGREDIENTS

300 g / 10 ½ oz / 1 ¾ cups couscous

1 red pepper, cubed

100 g / 3 ½ oz / 1 cup canned sweetcorn, drained

100 g / 3 ½ oz / ⅔ cup canned tuna, drained

a few chives to garnish

FOR THE DRESSING:

1 tsp runny honey

1 lime, juiced

3 tbsp olive oil

METHOD

1. Put the couscous in a serving bowl and pour over 300 ml of boiling water.

2. Cover the bowl with clingfilm and let it stand for 5 minutes then fluff up the grains with a fork.

3. Stir through the peppers, sweetcorn and tuna.

4. Whisk the honey with the lime juice then whisk in the olive oil.

5. Pour the dressing over the couscous and garnish with the chives.

Pumpkin and goat's cheese bruschetta

SERVES: 4 | PREP TIME: 10 MINUTES | COOKING TIME: 5-8 MINUTES

INGREDIENTS

flesh of 1 pumpkin, chopped into cubes

1 tbsp olive oil

3 slices wholemeal baguette

2 tbsp goat's cheese spread

1 handful basil leaves, washed

1 tsp sesame seeds

METHOD

1. Preheat the oven to 180°C (160° fan) / 355F / gas 4.

2. Coat the pumpkin cubes with olive oil and arrange evenly on a baking tray lined with greaseproof paper. Roast the pumpkin in the oven for just 5-8 minutes until it is soft but not browned.

3. Meanwhile, toast the slices of baguette under the grill at maximum heat for just a few minutes until lightly browned.

4. Once toasted, remove the slices of baguette from the grill and spread the goat's cheese on one side of each slice, then arrange the roasted pumpkin on top.

5. Sprinkle the basil leaves and sesame seeds on top and serve immediately, sprinkled with salt and pepper to taste.

Mini herb frittatas

MAKES: 12 | PREP TIME: 2 MINUTES | COOKING TIME: 15 MINUTES

INGREDIENTS

6 eggs

½ red onion, finely chopped

2 tbsp flat leaf parsley, finely chopped

2 tbsp chives, finely chopped

2 tbsp basil, finely chopped

METHOD

1. Preheat the oven to 180°C (160° fan) / 355F / gas 4.

2. Lightly beat the eggs and mix them with the onion and herbs, then season well with salt and pepper.

3. Pour the mixture into a 12-hole silicone cupcake mould and bake in the oven for 15 minutes or until the frittatas are set in the centre.

4. Serve warm or at room temperature.

Asparagus with dolcelatte cream

SERVES: 4 | PREP TIME: 10 MINUTES | COOKING TIME: 4-5 MINUTES

INGREDIENTS

400 g / 14 oz / 4 cups fresh asparagus
100 g / 3 ½ oz / 1 cup Dolcelatte, cubed
300 ml / 10 ½ fl. oz / 1 ½ cup double cream

METHOD

1. Snap the woody ends off the asparagus and cut the spears in half. Steam the asparagus for 5 minutes or until tender.

2. Meanwhile, put the Dolcelatte in a small saucepan with the cream and some freshly ground black pepper.

3. Bring to a gentle simmer, stirring constantly, then take off the heat.

4. Divide the asparagus between four warm plates and spoon over the sauce.

Red cabbage and apple salad

SERVES: 4 | PREPARATION TIME: 12 MINUTES

INGREDIENTS

1 lemon, juiced

4 tbsp olive oil

1 tsp coriander seeds, crushed

½ red cabbage, shredded

1 apple, cored and very thinly sliced

METHOD

1. Whisk together the lemon juice, olive oil and coriander seeds and toss with the cabbage.

2. Leave to stand for 10 minutes for the cabbage to soften then stir in the apple slices.

Goat's cheese and hazelnut canapés

MAKES: 20 | PREPARATION TIME: 10 MINUTES

INGREDIENTS

250 g / 9 oz / 1 ⅔ cups soft goat's cheese

55 g / 2 oz / ⅓ cup hazelnuts (cobnuts), chopped

METHOD

1. Divide the goat's cheese into 20 pieces and roll them into balls with your hands.

2. Roll the balls in the chopped hazelnuts to coat in an even layer then chill in the fridge until needed.

Radish and coriander salad

SERVES: 4 | PREPARATION TIME: 15 MINUTES

INGREDIENTS

200 g / 7 oz / 2 cups radishes

a small bunch fresh coriander (cilantro), roughly chopped

1 tbsp fish sauce

2 limes, juiced

1 tbsp caster (superfine) sugar

METHOD

1. Thinly slice the radishes with a sharp knife or mandolin and mix them with the coriander.

2. Stir the fish sauce and lime juice into the sugar until it dissolves then pour the dressing over the salad.

3. Wait for 10 minutes for the flavours to amalgamate before serving.

Potato and antipasti salad

SERVES: 2 | PREP TIME: 2 MINUTES | COOKING TIME: 12 MINUTES

INGREDIENTS

300 g / 10 ½ oz / 2 cups Maris Piper potatoes, peeled and thickly sliced

1 jar mixed vegetable antipasti in oil, drained and oil reserved

30 g Parmesan

a few sprigs basil

METHOD

1. Boil the potatoes in salted water for 12 minutes or until tender in the middle, then plunge into cold water to stop the cooking and drain well.

2. Toss the potatoes with the vegetable antipasti and dress with 2 tablespoons of the oil.

3. Use a vegetable peeler to shave over some Parmesan and garnish with basil.

Duck and mango salad

SERVES: 4 | PREP TIME: **10 MINUTES** | COOKING TIME: **5 MINUTES**

INGREDIENTS

1 large skinless duck breast, cut into thin strips

2 tbsp peanuts

1 tbsp vegetable oil

¼ Chinese cabbage, chopped

1 under-ripe mango, julienned

a small bunch of mint, leaves only

4 spring onions (scallions), sliced

FOR THE DRESSING:

1 tbsp caster (superfine) sugar

1 tbsp fish sauce

2 limes, juiced

1 tsp sesame oil

METHOD

1. Stir-fry the duck and peanuts in the vegetable oil for 5 minutes or until fully cooked through.

2. Toss the duck with the cabbage, mango, mint and spring onions.

3. Mix together the dressing ingredients and spoon them over the top.

Tuna and red pepper salad

SERVES: 4 | PREPARATION TIME: 5 MINUTES

INGREDIENTS

2 little gem lettuces, leaves separated

2 jars tuna in olive oil, drained and flaked

1 red pepper, diced

½ red onion, thinly sliced

50 g / 1 ¾ oz / ⅓ cup mixed olives

1 tbsp basil, chopped

4 tbsp extra virgin olive oil

2 hard-boiled eggs, halved

METHOD

1. Arrange the lettuce on four serving plates and arrange the tuna, peppers, onion and olives on top.

2. Scatter over the basil and dress with olive oil then garnish each plate with half a boiled egg.

Salt and pepper chicken

SERVES: 2 | PREP TIME: 2 MINUTES | COOKING TIME: 4 MINUTES

INGREDIENTS

2 tbsp vegetable oil

1 onion, sliced

200 g / 7 oz / 1 ½ cups chicken breast, sliced

½ tsp cayenne pepper

1 tsp ground Szechwan pepper

½ tsp caster (superfine) sugar

a small bunch of holy basil, leaves only

METHOD

1. Heat the oil in a wok and fry the onion and chicken for 4 minutes or until the chicken is cooked through.

2. Add the cayenne, Szechwan pepper and sugar with a pinch of salt then stir in the basil and cook until wilted.

3. Serve immediately.

Prawns with holy basil

SERVES: 2 | PREP TIME: 2 MINUTES | COOKING TIME: 5-8 MINUTES

INGREDIENTS

2 tbsp vegetable oil

2 cloves of garlic, skin on, squashed

1 red chilli, finely chopped

16 raw king prawns (shrimp), peeled leaving tails intact

1 tsp Szechwan peppercorns, crushed

½ tsp sea salt flakes

1 tsp granulated sugar

small bunch of holy basil, leaves only

METHOD

1. Heat the oil in a wok and fry the garlic cloves and chilli for 1 minute.

2. Add the prawns and stir-fry over a very high heat until just opaque then stir in the pepper, salt, sugar and basil.

3. Serve immediately.

Watermelon salad

SERVES: 2-4 | PREPARATION TIME: 15 MINUTES

INGREDIENTS

½ watermelon

1 small red onion, finely diced

a handful of mint leaves, chopped

1 tbsp extra virgin olive oil

1 tsp red wine vinegar

salt and freshly ground black pepper

2 tomatoes, chopped

100 g / 3 ½ oz feta, cut into cubes

METHOD

1. Cut the watermelon flesh away from the skin and remove the seeds. Cut into cubes and place into a large mixing bowl.

2. Mix the onion, mint, olive oil and vinegar in a small bowl. Season with salt and black pepper to taste and set aside for the flavours to combine.

3. Add the chopped tomatoes and feta cheese to the watermelon, mix to combine and season.

4. Pour the onions over the other ingredients and toss to coat.

5. Serve as a fresh salad or a side dish for fish or grilled meats.

Tuna sashimi and tomato salad

SERVES: 4 | PREP TIME: 20 MINUTES | COOKING TIME: 30 SECONDS

INGREDIENTS

200 g / 7 oz / 2 cups sushi-grade tuna loin

1 avocado, peeled and stoned

1 red onion, peeled and halved

FOR THE TOMATO SALAD:

6 tomatoes

1 tbsp rice wine vinegar (mirin)

1 tbsp rice vinegar

1 tsp caster (superfine) sugar

1 tsp sesame oil

METHOD

1. Score a cross in the top of the tomatoes and blanch them in boiling water for 30 seconds. When the skin of the tomatoes starts to curl up, remove them with a slotted spoon and dunk in a bowl of cold water.

2. Peel off and discard the skins then finely chop the tomato flesh. Mix together the mirin, vinegar, sugar and sesame oil and use it to dress the tomatoes.

3. Use a sharp knife to trim the tuna into 6 x 3 cm fillets, then cut it across the grain into 1 cm slices.

4. Slice the avocado and onion and arrange everything on four serving plates.

Couscous salad

SERVES: 4 | PREP TIME: 5 MINUTES | COOKING TIME: 5 MINUTES

INGREDIENTS

300 g / 10 ½ oz / 1 ¾ cup couscous

1 red pepper, cubed

1 green pepper, cubed

1 tomato, deseeded and cubed

2 tbsp mint, chopped

FOR THE DRESSING:

1 tsp runny honey

½ lemon, juiced

3 tbsp olive oil

METHOD

1. Put the couscous in a large serving bowl and pour over 300 ml of boiling water.

2. Cover the bowl with clingfilm and let it stand for 5 minutes then fluff up the grains with a fork.

3. Stir through the peppers, tomato and mint.

4. Whisk the honey with the lemon juice then whisk in the olive oil.

5. Pour the dressing over the couscous and serve.

Cucumber salad

SERVES: 4 | PREPARATION TIME: 5 MINUTES

INGREDIENTS

½ tsp mixed peppercorns

a pinch of chilli flakes

½ clove garlic

1 tbsp lemon juice

2 tbsp olive oil

3 tbsp Greek yogurt

1 cucumber, cut into batons

a small bunch of chives, chopped

a small bunch of flat leaf parsley, chopped

METHOD

1. Crush the peppercorns and chilli flakes with a pestle and mortar then add the garlic and a pinch of salt and grind to a paste.

2. Add the lemon juice, stirring with the pestle, followed by the oil, then stir in the yogurt.

3. Spoon the mixture into a serving bowl and toss with the cucumber and herbs.

Asparagus and parmesan salad

SERVES: 4 | PREP TIME: 5 MINUTES | COOKING TIME: 6 MINUTES

INGREDIENTS

200 g / 7 oz / 2 cups asparagus, trimmed

100 g / 3 ½ oz / 2 cups mixed salad leaves

100 g / 3 ½ oz / ⅔ cup cherry tomatoes, quartered

8 baby spring onions (scallions), halved lengthways

75 g / 2 ½ oz / ½ cup kalamata olives

2 tbsp sesame seeds

30 g Parmesan

a few sprigs of flowering thyme to garnish

FOR THE DRESSING:

1 tbsp mayonnaise

1 tbsp natural yogurt

1 tbsp lemon juice

1 tsp fresh thyme leaves, chopped

METHOD

1. Blanch the asparagus in boiling salted water for 6 minutes or until al dente. Plunge into cold water and drain well.

2. Divide the leaves between four plates and top with the asparagus, tomatoes, onions and olives.

3. Sprinkle over the sesame seeds and use a vegetable peeler to shave over some Parmesan.

4. Mix the dressing ingredients together and drizzle over the salad, then garnish with flowering thyme.

INDEX